Cooking for One

Cooking for One

Norah Mannion Wilmot

with sketches by the author

J. J. Douglas Ltd.
Vancouver, 1971

J.J. Douglas Ltd.
3645 McKechnie Drive
West Vancouver, British Columbia

Printed in Canada by Brock Webber Printing
Co. Ltd., Vancouver, British Columbia.

Contents

	Introduction and some Leftovers	7
I	Fish and Shellfish	11
II	Soups and Sauces	17
III	Seasoned Vinegars, Dressings and Salads	20
IV	Chickens Every Way	26
V	Egg, Omelettes and Soufflés	31
VI	Meats, Curries and Stews	37
VII	Vegetables	44
VIII	Entrées, Cheesies and Pancakes	48
IX	Desserts, Puddings and Pastries	51
X	Cakes and Cookies	54
XI	Breads and Buns	57
XII	Doctor's Orders	61
	Index	62

Introduction and some Leftovers

A three year old girl in our family referred to her mother as the "good cooker". It is not always easy to be a "good cooker" and it becomes even more difficult when you cook only for yourself. Many people when left alone, go through a period of tired indifference towards food and consequently drift into boredom and poor health. Yet an interesting and well-balanced dinner, whether it be at mid-day or evening, is a MUST.

This I discovered after months of "muddling": either settling for a boiled egg and toast or soup and a sandwich. And when I cooked a proper dinner for myself, I was confronted with a repitition of dull cold meats and heated-up vegetables. How I hated those pallid, little left-overs.

The recipes that follow have emerged from the diminution, dilution and sometimes improved formulae of everyday luncheon and dinner dishes culled from a manuscript cook book given to me fifty-seven years ago and from many glossy magazines. They have all been carefully tested and adjusted to the needs of one person and I have tried to make them interesting as well as nourishing.

The greatest difficulty in cooking for one is in the food shopping. This you will have to curtail or you will have wilted vegetables and dried up fruit etc. to contend with. Planning your meals and shopping twice a week will save endless waste and energy. Stock your larder with quick mixes, dehydrated soups, canned and frozen vegetables, meats and fish etc. You will find it more economical to buy frozen french fried potatoes and mushrooms in large bags and after you have shaken out what you required for a recipe, to tie up the corner of the bag and put in the refrigerator at once. Some packages may be divided and sealed in small "baggies".

Keep many tins—small tins—of quickly-prepared foods on hand, especially a small canned ham. A good dinner may be made out of a tin of macaroni with the addition of half a cup of good round or pork, seasoned and sauted until it crumbles.

A week's supply of fresh vegetables and fruit will keep in the refrigerator but leave room in the freezer compartment for a couple of loaves of your own home-made bread. Once you start to make your own bread you will never eat blown-up blotting paper again.

Whether you start from scratch or use prepared or pre-cooked foods, the seasoning is most important so make sure that you have a good range of your favourite seasons and condiments in little bottles. And always keep on hand a fresh lemon, some parsley, a few green onions and a pepper grinder.

You will find recipes here to enable you to make your own seasoned vinegars, French, Italian, etc. And your own croutons. Always use butter in any recipe which calls for "shortening", also for broiling, baking and sauteing. Nothing can replace the flavour and elegance that good dairy butter gives to everything. For cooking wines, I use sherry and a dry Sauterne. You can of course use "hard lickers" on occasion and for such personal seasoning you have to use your own judgement as to the quantity to be used.

Buy coffee beans and grind them to your size. "Filter" is my choice and I transfer coffee to pint sealers and keep in the refrigerator.

Don't be afraid to use your imagination and experiment. For instance, if you are deadly sick of peanut butter sandwiches, try instead whole cashews and seasoning salt — I find "Johnny's" wonderful. You don't need dressing but butter the bread well. Or if you are having a soup and salad dinner, try heating a tin of consomme or beef bouillon with a good dash of sherry — no other dilution is necessary. Bouillon, seasoned and with sherry added may be served ice cold.

And if you have to live alone, why not have good working conditions with less work involved? The washing up of those family-sized pots and pans is most discouraging when you are cooking in small quantities. So sort out that jungle of cooking utensils in your kitchen and only keep the smallest of everything. The Salvation Army love big old pots and pans.

Invest in a few new ones. If you do not have one of those small cast iron skillets by all means buy one. A six inch size is almost a necessity for pan-broiling your small steaks, chops, etc. A new one will have to be seasoned but that is easily done by heating in it two or three tablespoons of cooking oil until it smokes. Allow it to cool for some hours and repeat the process. It then should be wiped out with paper towelling and is ready for use. Do not clean it by scouring with cleaning powders but simply wash it when necessary and keep wiped out with paper. It will develop a smooth, black surface and will not stick.

There is a very hard-baked, white cooking ware that is wonderful for the lone cook for it can be taken from the refrigerator to the hot stove top or oven without fear of damage.

A five inch square casserole is most useful particularly for top stove cooking and it fits the tiny oven in the new-type toaster called the "TOAST-R-OVEN". If you need a new toaster, do have one of these. It takes up little more room than a pop-up toaster and is not very much more costly. It will do everything but broil and I use one for baking puddings, casseroles, muffins, biscuits as well as meats and fish. And it saves on power.

A coffee pot in a three cup size is ideal, particularly if it is of the same hard-baked, white ware as you can then put it on direct heat. With the addition of a cheap, plastic filter and a size 101 MELITTA filterpaper, you can have in seconds the most delicious coffee and you will never go back to "INSTANT" coffee.

Last of all, for your own comfort, have some of those wonderful, new, plastic turn-tables. They come in many sizes, single and double deckers and are such inexpensive space savers that no civilized kitchen should be without them. Use one in your spice and condiment cupboard and as revolving platforms in your refrigerator, they avoid much waste in forgotten and pushed back jars, opened cans, etc. A large, double one will hold endless cans and packages in your storage shelf and a large, single one in that hateful, under-the-sink place will transform it into a wonder of convenience, save backaches and many curses.

I almost called this little book COOK ALONE AND LIKE IT. I hope that it helps you to do just that.

Good luck.
NORAH MANNION WILMOT

Easy Prune Pudding

1/2 pkg. (1/3 cup) Lemon flavoured gelatin
1 to 1/2 teaspoons grated rind
1 egg white stiffly beaten with 1 tsp. sugar
Serve with custard sauce.

Ketchup

1 — 46 oz. tomato juice
1/2 cup white wine vinegar
garlic powder
artificial sweetener to taste

Bring to a boil and simmer uncovered until thick, stirring occasionally. Cook down to 1/3 the volume

Sweet & Sour Liver — 1 serving

1 1/4 cups tomato juice
1/4 " fresh pineapple cubed or Dole Pineapple in can
2 tsps. chives
1 tablespoon vinegar
2 tsps. soy sauce
sweetener to equal 4 tsps sugar or to taste
1 beef bouillon cube
1/2 medium green pepper diced
8 oz. liver

Combine all ingredients except liver in a sauce pan. Simmer uncovered 20 minutes. Add liver & cook 5 to 7 mins. Do not overcook.

9

I

Fish and Shellfish

According to statistics published by the Dept. of Fisheries, Ottawa, Canada, nearly all fish have a higher protein value than beef, veal, or pork. Fish, & especially Shellfish, in the diet of persons inclined to be anaemic are very valuable and easy to digest.

Fresh fish in season is definitely more desirable than frozen, especially salmon, so let us follow the seasons. Care should be taken not to over cook any kind of fish. Too much cooking makes it dry and tasteless.

Many types of frozen fish are always available but are more difficult to divide for one person. Frozen fish cakes divide easily for one serving.

Most of us dislike washing fishy pans and hate the smell of cooking or broiling. This can be avoided by making a little "throw-away" pan of heavy duty foil. A slice, or fillets, etc. can be broiled, baked, or oven poached in one of these and one has no smelly pan to wash.

Use a piece of heavy duty foil two inches larger than the piece of fish; turn up a good inch to form a little pan and fold in corners. Place this on a foil pie plate or pan large enough to support it when taking out of oven or broiler.

BROILED SOLE

1 fillet, big enough for one; 1 tsp. soft butter; I tbsp. lemon juice; salt, pepper to taste; 1/8 tsp. powdered sweet basil; 3 drops Worcester Sauce.

Prepare your "throw-away" broil pan and place fish on buttered surface.   (Skin side down). Rub all over with the soft butter and sprinkle with salt, pepper and basil, pour the lemon juice and Worcester sauce over all and another little sprinkle of salt.

Place tin about five inches under heated broiler and cook about five minutes. It is not necessary to turn a thin fillet.

This is nice with green beans, frenched, and mashed potato (Instant is handy for one), and sliced field ripened tomatoes. (Slice a fair sized tomato in three or four slices, with finely chopped green onion in between. Sprinkle with a little sugar, salt and vinegar or lemon juice) Delicious!!!!!

Any cooked fish is improved with a little finely chopped parsley. Put it over the top of your seasoned fish before broiling.

BROILED FRESH SALMON SLICE

Butter both sides of fish and season with: freshly ground pepper; ½ tsp. salt; sprinkle with: 1 tbsp, lemon juice; 1 tbsp. finely chopped parsley.

Place in little prepared "throw-away" foil pan with supporting pan under it and broil for three minutes or more, according to thickness of fish — turn and broil for three minutes more. Pan should be placed five inches below heat.

BREADING TIP

There is a new way of breading fish, chicken, veal, etc., that seems to insure a tender, moist baked finish and requires no greased pan.

Use *evaporated milk,* instead of the usual beaten egg and water.

Pour out half a very small tin of milk on a dinner plate, season to taste with salt, paprika, pepper, etc.

Have ready a cup of finely rolled *corn flakes.* Dip fish fillets or slices in corn flakes, then in milk, back to corn flakes, coating well in the usual manner of breading. Now, place your pieces of fish on a square of foil, bring up the sides to almost cover it and bake for twenty minutes or so, according to thickness of fish.

Fish may be sprinkled with lemon juice and a little sherry when removed from oven. (This is also a splendid way of baking many other things — cut-up chicken, veal, etc.) Can be covered part of the time, but takes a much longer time to cook.

FISH CAKES

¾ c. mashed potato (Instant o.k.); ½ c. of left-over fresh or canned fish; season to taste; 1 sm. egg, beaten.

Mix together, make into two flat cakes, dip into flour and saute in a little butter until brown on both sides and well heated through. These are nice with a little chili sauce and 2 or 3 slices of broiled bacon.

FILLET OR SLICE OF FISH

1 tbsp. butter; 1 tbsp. lemon juice;
Salt, pepper; 1 tbsp. fine parsley.

Place fish, seasonings and lemon juice in piece of heavy foil. Draw up and wrap to seal carefully so that no juice escapes. "Drugstore" wrap. Place parcel in a casserole or pan containing a half inch of hot water. Bake 15 to 20 minutes in 350 oven. (According to thickness of fish.) When parcel is opened the fish will be found swimming in its own juices. This makes a delicious sauce or may be poured over fish and served at once. Parsley added.

SCALLOPS — BREADED

¼ lb. scallops, fresh or frozen; 1 egg beaten lightly; add: ½ tsp. salt; ¼ tsp. accent; ¼ tsp. freshly ground pepper; ½ tsp. worcester sauce.

Mix well: Scald scallops and let stand for 5 minutes. Drain. On a piece of waxed paper, have at least a cupful of fine dry bread crumbs or crushed corn flakes. Roll scallops first in crumbs then dip into seasoned egg and again into crumbs. Heat two tablespoons of butter on skillet and cook scallops until tender, turning them and sauteing until nicely brown, about five minutes, according to size. Nice with tartar sauce.

CURRIED SCALLOPS

¼ lb. scallops, fresh or frozen; 3 green onions minced; ¼ tsp. salt; ¼ tsp. accent; dash of pepper and nutmeg; ¼ tsp. celery salt; 2 tsp. curry; ¼ tsp. "Spice Island" Sea-food seasoning; 1 tbsp. butter; 1 c. milk; 1 tbsp. flour.

Heat butter and add onions, saute for a few minutes and add all the seasonings and flour. Stir until it boils. Add the scallops which you have let stand in boiling water for two or three minutes. Cook slowly until they are bubbling, about ten minutes. They should not be over cooked as it makes them tough.

If you think sauce is too thick before you add the scallops, a little water may be added.

Serve with boiled rice or instant rice.

FRIED OYSTERS   GOURMET

½ a small carton fresh oysters; 1 tbsp. butter; 1 tbsp. lemon juice; seasonings, salt and pepper; ¼ c. chili sauce; fine bread crumbs or corn meal; liquid from oysters.

Roll oysters in seasoned crumbs or corn meal. Saute in hot melted butter until the edges curl. Add lemon juice, chili sauce and more salt if necessary. Cover and simmer for a few minutes until cooked and piping hot.

FRIED OYSTERS WITH BACON

2 slices bacon; ½ small carton oysters; seasoning; flour.

Cook bacon slowly until crisp. Remove from pan. Roll oysters in seasoned flour and saute in hot bacon fat until edges curl and they are cooked through. 2 or 3 drops of Worcester sauce may be added. Garnish with bacon and a wedge of lemon.

UNCOMPLICATED SCALLOPED OYSTERS

½ box of fresh or frozen oysters; ½ c. oyster liquor and milk combined; ½ c. rolled cracker crumbs; 2 tbsp. butter; salt and pepper.

Use part of butter to grease small flat casserole. Sprinkle with half the fine crumbs. Put oysters in (season with salt and pepper). Dot with butter and add the oyster juice and milk. Cover with remaining crumbs and dot with the rest of the butter, a little salt, pepper, and paprika. Bake for 20 min. in 375 oven.

OYSTERS — GOURMET BUT QUICK

½ carton fresh or frozen oysters; ¼ c. fine bread or cracker crumbs; ¼ tsp. salt; dash of ground pepper; 2 tbsp. melted butter; 1 tsp. snipped parsley; ½ can cream of mushroom or celery soup, diluted with liquid from oysters (at least 2 tbsp.)

Combine crumbs, butter and seasonings. Heat soup and liquid to boiling point. Add oysters and cook until edges curl. Place half crumbs in hot buttered small casserole. Add oysters and soup mixture. Top with remaining crumbs. Place casserole in broiler (5" from top) for a few minutes to brown slightly. Have this with a tossed salad and heated tea biscuits.

CLAM CHOWDER

This recipe makes two generous servings. It is even better if kept in refrigerator for 24 hours. Butter or razor clams are the best. Do not use those "Baby" clams; they have no flavour.

1 ten oz. can clams, 2 c. milk, 1 slice bacon, cut in ¼" bits; 1 med. sized onion, minced; 1 med. sized potato, diced; salt and pepper to taste; 1 c. boiling water and clam juice; 1 tbsp. butter; 1 tbsp. flour.

Fry bits of bacon until nearly cooked; drain off most of fat and saute onions until pale yellow, add a cup of boiling water, the juice from clams and the diced potatoes. Season and cook the potatoes until firm but not mushy. In a larger pot melt the butter, blend in the flour, add the milk gradually and bring to a boil. Add the drained clams (Cut in pieces) and the first mixture. Stir this and cook together until piping hot. More seasoning may be added and a little garlic is optional.

Note: 2 or 3 crackers rolled finely and butter added, may be used instead of the flour in thickening.

Fresh crab-meat and shrimps are so delicious with salt, pepper and a dash of lemon juice that it seems a shame to be-devil them up into fussy casseroles and over dressed salads. Try it some time. Serve on a lone leaf of lettuce for charm.

CURRY SAUCE

This simple sauce may be used with any kind of fish, fresh or canned. A small tin of shrimps, lobster, crab, or salmon, (with juice), may be added to this recipe and served with rice.

1 small onion or three green ones; ¼ c. minced celery; 1½ tbsp. melted butter; 1 tbsp. flour; ½ tsp. salt, pepper; 1 to 2 tsp. curry; 1 c. milk.

Mince the onion and celery and saute lightly in the melted butter. Add the curry, salt and flour. Stir and add the milk gradually until mixture thickens. Add small tin of fish with *all* the juice and heat to boiling point. Simmer slowly and avoid breaking up fish by too much stirring. A little powdered garlic and ginger may be added if desired. Do not use juice from tuna — it is too oily.

CREAMED FISH OF ANY KIND

This may be made quickly by using a half tin of mushroom, celery or any creamed soup, but the best way is to use my recipe for home-made mushroom soup. Heat one cup of soup and add 1 smallest tin of fish. Try not to break it up too much: Season to taste and let it simmer until it comes to a boil. Serve in a pre-baked patty shell or on a slice of very thin buttered toast. I always add the juice of any canned fish, excepting tuna, to whatever I am making.

HOT WEATHER SUPPER

½ a fairly large avocado, 1 small tin of shrimps or crab; Sharp French dressing; 1 tbsp. Sea-food Sauce; lettuce.

Cut avocado in half length wise and remove pit. Wrap one half with Saran or such and return to refrigerator. Sprinkle well with salt and lemon juice put in the drained shrimps or crab and put a good blob of following dressing on top.

SEA FOOD DRESSING WITH AVOCADO

1/3 cup commercial sour cream; 1 tsp. any seasoned vinegar you prefer; 1 finely minced green onion or 1 tsp. grated onion; ¼ cup pepper sauce; 2 drops Worcester sauce; 1 Tbsp. parsley.

A teaspoon of sharp Fr. dressing should be sprinkled over the pear before adding fish. Avocado pear needs lots of salt as it is very smug without it. Serve on crisp lettuce.

CRAB NORAHBURG

May also be made with lobster or shrimps.

> *1 tbsp. butter; ¼ tsp. salt; a little accent, and ground pepper; 2*
> *green onions thinly sliced; ¼ cup fresh or frozen mushrooms;*
> *½ cup light cream or rich milk; liquid from 1 small tin of crab;*
> *1 tbsp. instant potato flakes; 1 small egg; 1 tsp. sherry; Garlic*
> *flavoured croutons, Parmesan Cheese, 1 tbsp. chopped parsley.*

In small heavy skillet, saute in butter the onions, celery and sliced mushrooms three min., add crab liquid and "creamy", heat, add seasonings and potato flakes. Stir to boiling point add the crab meat and heat. Take off heat and add the well beaten egg. Try not to break up the crab meat too much and transfer to small buttered casserole; sprinkle with sherry and cover with broken up croutons and a sifting of packaged Parmesan cheese. Brown in 350 oven until set.

This with sliced tomatoes makes an excellent hot weather meal.

II

Soups and Sauces

There are so many wonderful dehydrated soups on the market that the lone "cooker" will be advised to use them: a package can be divided and liquid added according to the appetite. Always shake package well to blend the seasonings before dividing and follow directions please.

In using canned soups use smallest cans for one serving. If you have only the 10 oz. size it may be diluted using a *half* tin of water or milk instead of the whole tin. This makes a nourishing luncheon or supper.

Consomme or beef boullion need not be diluted at all except for a couple of tbsp. of sherry as a "Pick-me-up". Try it some tired time.

Among the dehydrated soups there is a "Garden Vegetable Soup Mix" that cannot be improved on. Think of all the work in home made vegetable soup as our Grandmothers made it.

Home made Mushroom or Cream of Asparagus soup is better than the canned varieties and not as flat and uninteresting. If you use the canned it will bear a lot of "personal seasoning".

BASIC CREAM SOUP

Home made cream soups are an excellent base for the small casserole or "top stove dish".

If you are having asparagus or boiled celery save the water, steal a couple of stalks of either, chop finely and add to soup.

1½ tbls. butter, 1 cup veg. water, 1½ tbls. flour, salt,
accent and pepper.

Cook together until blended, add the vegetable juice, simmer until thick and add a cup of milk or a little more, (gradually) stir until thick. A tbls. grated onion and some chopped parsley may be added to this and will be an improvement.

Any left over creamed soup may be saved and with a little extra seasoning, curry, etc. added to whatever one wants to make in to a creamed dish or small casserole. A few crumbs, a little grated cheese and you have a gourmet production. Use your imagination. How about a quarter of a glass of sauterne and a half teasp. of Spice Island Sea-food flavouring for any dish with canned or fresh fish in it???

CREAM OF MUSHROOM SOUP

This is much nicer than any canned variety and can be used as a foundation for a casserole or any creamed dish.

½ c. fresh mushrooms; 1 fat green onion (White part) 1 small piece heart celery; 1 chicken boullion cube; 1 c. boiling water; 1 c. top milk or part "creamy" — or 1 small tin of evaporated milk; 1 tbsp. butter; 1 tbsp. flour; seasoning, salt, pepper; 1 tsp. finely minced parsley.

Mince the mushrooms, onion and celery. Put them in a quart sized pot and add a cup of boiling water, the chicken cube and all seasonings and simmer for 3 minutes.

Cream butter and flour together, add to above mixture and stir and cook until it thickens. Add the cup of milk gradually, stirring carefully until it comes to a boil. Serve with a little minced parsley and paprika sprinkled on top. Keep half of it to make a creamed dish or small casserole the next day. (If you are hungry you will eat it all!)

SOUR CREAM AND CAPER SAUCE

1 tbsp. crushed capers;
a little salt and cayenne;
½ c. commercial sour cream.

Mix and chill. Can be used on cold fish or added to a baked fillet of fish at the last and not chilled.

ORANGE SOUR CREAM SAUCE

½ c. sour cream; 1 tbsp. freshly grated orange;
pinch of salt; 1 tsp. sugar; 2 drops angostura bitters.

This is delicious on a fruit salad.

SOUR CREAM MAYONNAISE

½ c. sour cream; 2 drops angostura bitters;
1 good tbsp. seasoned mayonnaise.

Mix and use for a fruit salad or anything you happen to assemble, tomatoes, egg halves, chopped celery, etc., etc., etc.

SEAFOOD SAUCE WITH SOUR CREAM

1 tbsp. butter; 1 tbsp. lemon juice; 1 tbsp. finely chopped green onion; ½ c. cooking Sauterne; ½ tsp. Spice Island Seafood Season; ½ c. commercial sour cream or yogurt.

Put everything but the sour cream in a small pan and boil until reduced to *half* the quantity. *Cool* and when it is quite cold stir in sour cream. Adjust seasoning if necessary.

This sauce may also be served hot over any cooked fish. Let the foundation cool slightly, add the sour cream and let it heat well, but do not allow it to boil.

INSTANT CHEESE SAUCE

Quick cheese sauce for one may be made instantly by mixing: 1 tbsp. cheese whiz with 2 tbsp. milk, or cream. Stir together and heat it in tiny sauce pan and season with salt and pepper and a speck of dry mustard.

ALMOST INSTANT CHEESE SAUCE

2 tbsp. grated old cheese; speck of cayenne;
2 tbsp. Evaporated Milk;
1 tbsp. mayonnaise, see recipe.

Heat in smallest pan, the evaporated milk and cheese until blended. Take off stove for a moment and stir in mayonnaise, pepper and a drop of Angostura bitters (optional). Return to heat, but not to boil. Have your big dinner plate ready with your hot meat and vegetables on it and immediately pour over the broccoli or cauliflower, the piping hot sauce. I am taking it for granted that most of us who live alone have our dinner on one big hot dinner plate. Saves extra dishes and tempers.

CUCUMBER SAUCE

¼ c. chopped cucumber, drained;
¼ c. sour cream; 1 tsp. lemon juice;
salt, pepper and paprika.

Mix and chill before serving with any kind of fish. Also good with a vegetable salad.

PARSLEY

Parsley may be added to any fish sauce or meat dish, chicken etc. it adds zest, color and vitamins.

Parsley stems may be crushed and used to tint butter or margarine a lovely green.

III

Seasoned Vinegars, Dressings and Salads

SEASONED VINEGARS

I am starting this chapter with the seasoned vinegars, as I use them in all salad dressings and in anything that calls for vinegar. Some of these are out of the ordinary and my own ideas. They lend a quite different and tantalizing flavour to many things.Use *"pure cider vinegar"* for all of these recipes. Pint bottles lend uniformity to your spice and condiment shelf or plastic turntable.

NASTURTIUM VINEGAR — *Original Recipe*

1 c. tender young nasturtium seeds (crushed); a few stalks and leaves cut very finely; 1 tsp. salt; 1 tsp. sugar; 3 drops pepper sauce; ¼ tsp. dry mustard; 2 c. cider vinegar

Borrow or steal the seeds, etc. Boil vinegar and seasonings for a minute or two and pour over the nasturtium items. Allow to come to a boil and let stand until perfectly cold. Let this stand (covered) for several days and strain and bottle it.

TARRAGON VINEGAR — *Original Recipe*

If you can get fresh tarragon, strip leaves and crush or chop: 1 c. tarragon leaves, cover with 2 c. boiling vinegar, add 1 tsp. salt, 1 tsp. sugar.

Let stand for a few days, strain and bottle. The same procedure may be followed for making many different vinegars, using the dried herbs,(powdered as in the little bottles), a teaspoon or two to a pint of vinegar, etc.

GARLIC VINEGAR

4 or 5 cloves of fresh garlic;
2 c. cold cider vinegar; 1 tsp. salt;
1 tsp. tobasco; 1 tsp. sugar;

Crush garlic and add to other ingredients. Let stand for two weeks in covered jar. Strain and bottle in pint vinegar bottle. Wonderful in different salad dressings - French, Italian, etc.

PAPAYA SEED VINEGAR

1 pint pure cider vinegar; 1 tsp. salt;
1 tsp. sugar; seeds from one papaya

This is an original recipe.

Cut the papaya in two, lengthwise, shake out the seeds or remove with a fork to a dinner plate. Be careful not to have any pulp or stringy bits: Crush seeds a little with a fork. Boil the vinegar, salt, and sugar for a few minutes. Add the seeds, transfer to a sealer and let stand at room temperature for ten days. Strain through a piece of cheese cloth and put in pint vinegar bottle.

This is quite different from any of the various flavoured vinegars and adds piquancy to any salad dressing, curried dish, etc. Of course you will have the delicious fruit for breakfast, serve quite cold and sprinkle a little salt and a squeeze of lemon or lime juice.

USE: Basil Vinegar — for tomato, potato or egg; Marjoram Vinegar — in green salads; Dill, Nasturtium or Papaya seed — in any fish salad; Garlic Vinegar — to your own discretion.

CHUTNEY VINEGAR

2 tbsp. from that nice big expensive bottle of Indian Chutney, chopped finely, and add: 1½ c. hot cider vinegar. Bottle — do not strain.

SOUR CREAM DRESSING

This may be prepared in minutes.
For One —

½ c. sour cream (commercial); 1 tsp. lemon juice; 1 tsp. any seasoned vinegar you prefer; 1 tsp. grated onion or 1 green onion minced; ¼ tsp. salt; ¼ tsp. sugar; ¼ tsp. chili powder; 2 drops Worcester Sauce.

Mix and chill a few minutes.

May be used on: sliced tomatoes, avocado, any small tin of fish, etc.

COMMERCIAL "REAL MAYONNAISE"

This can be made more interesting and much less dull and smug if doctored up a little.

To a middle sized jar, this is what I do: Take a cup full, or so, out of jar and mix in the following — replace in jar and with a long spoon stir it well from bottom and mix all thoroughly 2 tsp. papaya or nasturtium vinegar, or any seasoned one you prefer.

1 tsp. lemon juice; ¼ tsp. salt;
½ tsp. grated fresh orange; ¼ tsp. dry mustard;
a few drops of Tobasco or Pepper sauce.

Papaya or Nasturium Vinegar lend special enchantment to any salad dressing. Garlic vinegar is optional.

BASIC FRENCH OR ITALIAN DRESSING

1/3rd quantity of flavoured vinegar;
2/3rds quantity of oil

Season to taste with salt, dry mustard, sugar and paprika, or you may use 1 part vinegar or 1 lemon to 3 parts oil or again if you like a sharper dressing use half vinegar and half oil. Adding what seasoning you like the best. Crushed fresh garlic can be added with basic seasonings and a multitude of other things. One made with lemon and orange juice intead of vinegar is refreshing on fruit salads.

SALADS

There are literally hundreds that the lone "Cooker" may make for one serving. The Magazines are full of the most gorgeous and appetizing ones. It is all a matter of arrangement and choice of materials. *The Tossed Salad* with its beauti-shades of green and the many shrimp, crab, avocado jellied jobs give us an endless choice.

French, Italian and many other liquid dressings may be made at home and are as good if not better than the small expensive bottles.

Lettuce is difficult for many people to digest and need only be served as a garnish for any of the following old standbys.

BEET AND CELERY

This salad keeps for several days.

1 c. diced pickled beets; 1 c. chopped celery; 1 green onion (or slice of small onion), chopped finely; Salad dressing of your choice; Season with a little garlic powder, if liked and celery salt.

Left over fresh beets may be substituted for canned or pickled beets.

APPLE AND CELERY

dice large juicy apple;
dice 2 tender stocks of celery (de-stringed).

Mix with a teaspoon of lemon juice and 2 tbsp. thick mayonnaise of your choice. A green onion, chopped is optional.

AUNT LIZZIE'S CHICKEN SALAD

This recipe for Chicken Salad has been in our family for nearly a century. It is simple and delicious and has remained untrammelled throughout the years. (Reduced to 1 serving)

¾ c. chicken, cut in ¼" pieces;
½ c. celery, chopped — freshly ground pepper;
slight sprinkle of salt;
add: ¼ c. mayonnaise.

NOTHING ELSE: Stir all together. White meat was generally used and crisp hearts of celery and the mayonnaise was homemade in the usual way, of adding the oil drop by drop to egg yolk, salt and pepper, thinning with lemon juice or vinegar, or old fashioned boiled dressing was used. It was served on lettuce with no garnishments whatever. Try it with some "Real Mayonnaise" — doctored my way.

POTATO SALAD

As this salad keeps for several days, if kept covered in refrigerator, it is advisable to make enough for two or three times.

The principal rule in making a really good potato salad is to boil the potatoes, with skin on, peel and cut in ½" cubes.

Place these in a shallow bowl, while hot, and, at once, pour over them a cup full of french dressing OR a cup of homemade "Boiled Dressing" OR a cup of commercial Cold Slaw dressing. Cool.

According to proportion you are making, add chopped green onions and celery heart (dash of garlic is optional) and finely chopped parsley.

If you are using it all at once, add cucumber cut in chunks and chopped hard boiled eggs. Otherwise, use them for a garnish. Serve on crisp lettuce.

OLD STANDBY — COTTAGE CHEESE AND FRUIT

Place three or four leaves of crisp lettuce on a large dinner plate. Mound a cup of fresh cottage cheese in the middle. Surround with fruit of your choice. If you have this salad very often, open several tins of fruit, transfer to pint sealers and fish out what you want from day to day.

a slice of pineapple; a large half peach;
a whole apricot; a half pear; a few green grapes.

Wedges of an unpeeled red apple add attraction. Pour over this the salad dressing you like best. Sour cream mixed with a ½ tsp. lemon juice, a tbsp. of the fruit juices, and a little "Real" mayonnaise (seasoned up my way) or any of the french dressings you might like, and so on.

I like French dressing made with seasoned vinegar on Fruit Salad!

HAM AND EGG SALAD

1 thick slice from a small canned ham, cut in small cubes and sprinkled with: ¼ tsp. dry mustard; add: ¼ c. chopped celery; 2 green onions, finely chopped; 1 hard boiled egg, sliced and pepped up with a little seasoned salt or "Salad Elegance" (Johnny's); Combine all and toss with: ¼ c. Commercial "Real Mayonnaise" (Doctored). (See recipe for "Salad Dressings").
Serve on a bed of crisp lettuce.

EASY SALAD SUPPER

For a hot weather meal: some crisp lettuce; 1 smallest tin of: salmon, crab, shrimp or lobster (the last is gold-plated); 1 tbsp. "Real" mayonnaise or "Sea-food" sauce with sour cream (see salad dressings).

Drain fish and pile on lettuce leaves. Top with a good splash of salad dressing, sprinkle with paprika and a little finely chopped parsley and you have a delicious luncheon. Perhaps you will want to garnish it with a piece of dill pickle and a slice or two of hard boiled egg. (Slices of hard boiled egg are deadly dull, unless sprinkled with a little seasoned salt or "Johnny's Salad Elegance" and a dash of any herb vinegar, or lemon juice.

CORNED BEEF SALAD SUPPER

This may be made the night before and chilled.

1/3rd package lemon jello or gelatine; 1/3 cup boiling water; 2 tsp. flavoured vinegar; ground pepper, a little salt; ¼ tsp. Worcester sauce.

Mix above ingredients together, stir to dissolve and cool.
When quite cold but not set add the following

¼ cup diced celery heart; two green onions finely diced; 1 hard boiled egg, diced and seasoned; ½ small tin of corned beef cubed.

Toss all together and put in a small mould.
When chilled and set, it may be turned out on a bed of torn up lettuce and served with horse radish sauce.

Horse Radish Sauce

1 tbsp. Mayonnaise;
1 tbsp. commercial Sour Cream;
1 tbsp. prepared horse radish;
a little salt and freshly ground pepper.

24

TOMATOES

TOMATOES according to Aunt Lizzie's memories, were almost unknown a hundred years ago.

At first the beautiful scarlet "love apple", as it was called, was only brought in and placed upon the mantel piece to be admired. Later, Aunt Lizzie speaks of serving a platter of sliced ripe tomatoes with cold turkey supper.

Tomatoes should *always* be kept and served at room temperature.

TOMATOES — NATURE'S BEST

Peel and slice tomatoes (Room Temperature). Sprinkle with a little sugar, salt and lemon juice. Add absolutely nothing else and you will have the true flavour of delicious sun-ripened tomatoes.

DRESSED UP TOMATOES

Peel, and slice 1 large or 2 small tomatoes (according to capacity). Sprinkle with a little sugar and salt; Sprinkle with: 1 gr. onion, minced; ¼ c. diced celery (white); ½ tsp. snipped parsley; Dribble on a little of any preferred french dressing.

Serve on shredded lettuce.

HOME MADE CROUTONS

Four slices of two or three day old bread half an inch thick. Trim crusts off into neat squares. Score one side lightly (do not cut through)

Spread lightly with soft butter, seasoned to your taste.

Place whole slices on cookie sheet and toast in 350 oven until light bown. (About 10 min.) When cool, break them apart in neat squares. Store in a tin box or sealer.

Parmesan Cheese (packaged) may be sprinkled over half the slices before toasting.

SEASONED BUTTER

3 or 4 tbsp. soft butter; ½ tsp. of any favourite herb; ½ tsp. salt; ½ tsp. pepper sauce; ½ tsp. garlic powder or one clove crushed; ¼ tsp. celery salt.

Cream all together and add anything else you like.

Many different kinds of croutons may be made by varying the seasonings. The bread may be cut in cubes and tossed in the melted seasoned butter before baking. I like my way the best.

IV

Chickens Every Way

Poultry seems much too elegant a heading for this chapter — specially when one views those trays of pale slippery looking "chicken parts" or even the whole fryers all puffed out with their little bags of "innards". They are so often tasteless and stringy.

When I was newly married an old lady from Macon, Georgia advised me to "always look for a *fat yaller chicken; never* buy one of those blue ones". Ever since that I have poked around the hanging fowl and can usually come up with a fairly fat yellow one.

Chicken lends itself to many ways of "Cooking for one" and is the cheapest meat on the market.

There are many ways of doing chicken for one person. The new style corn-crisp method lends itself to slices of fish, pork chops or veal cutlet as well.

This definitely calls for EVAPORATED MILK. Keep smallest tins of milk on hand. Pour out a half cup and seal up the tin. It will keep for a few days and can be used in a cheese omelette or many things.

Season your portion of milk with salt, pepper, paprika, a little accent or whatever herb you prefer; spread on a plate and marinate chicken, etc. in this for a few minutes. Roll in slightly crushed cornflakes, and let stand for a few minutes; place on a piece of heavy foil in a baking dish or pan — do not crowd. No shortening is required. If a less crisp crust is desired a piece of foil may be put loosely on top.

Chicken will take forty minutes or so, pork a little longer and fish (according to thickness) 20 minutes or longer. It should be moist and tender inside. The evaporated milk takes the place of butter or shortening and the cornflakes seals the flavour.

Bake in pre-heated 325 oven.

FRICASSEE OF CHICKEN

From half a chicken, cut off: Neck, drumstick and wing. Wash thoroughly. 1 tsp. salt; ¼ tsp. ground pepper; 1/8 tsp. rosemary; 1 thin slice lemon; 1 med. sized onion, sliced; ¼ c. chopped celery and tops; 1 pint boiling water (More if necessary).

Bring all ingredients except chicken to a boil, add chicken parts and simmer slowly for 40 minutes, or so, (until tender).

Thick potato slices may be added, a few minutes before it is quite cooked and one has a complete meal.

It is not necessary to thicken all the broth. Pour off a mug or so and reserve for soup or "Chicken a la King and thicken remainder with 2 tsp. flour, 2 tsp. butter, blended with ½ cup of lukewarm broth. Stir until it boils and enjoy a quickly prepared and complete meal.

FRIED CHICKEN — OLD FASHIONED

Rinse chicken part in cold water and dry on a paper towel; place on plate and rub it all over with half a lemon — squeeze on the juice and let it stand for a few minutes. Place seasoned flour in paper bag and shake chicken until it is thoroughly coated. Saute in a tablespoon *butter* until brown on both sides and bake in 350 oven for forty minutes or so (until fork tender). May be covered part of the time.

FRIED CHICKEN — MODERN WAY

Evaporated milk *must* be used for this method. Ordinary milk or cream simply will not do. Using part of a very small tin of evaporated milk, dip chicken part and pat it over all surfaces. Roll in season crushed corn flakes and proceed as in above recipe.

This may also be wrapped *loosely* in foil and baked. It will be tender and moist despite its crisp covering. The evaporated milk takes the place of shortening and the cornflakes seal in the flavour.

Fowl, Meat, or Fish may be done this same way.

GINGERY LEGS AND THIGHS

This recipe was obtained in Honolulu, sounds a little immoral but is delicious and easy to make.

chicken portions for one; 1 tbsp. soy sauce;
½ tsp. powdered ginger; ½ tsp. sugar;
¼ tsp. salt; 1 tsp. grated raw orange peel.

Marinate chicken in soy sauce and all seasonings. Roll in corn meal and saute in butter. Pan may be covered part time. Cook gently, either on stove top or in oven until crisp and tender.

MAKESHIFT LAZY CHICKEN

Chicken parts for one;
½ tin of undiluted cream of mushroom soup;
add seasoning and snipped parsley, etc.

Saute chicken parts in a little butter until nearly cooked. Place in a small casserole. Cover with soup which has been seasoned enough to take off the dull, flat taste of most creamed soups. Sprinkle with fine bread crumbs and a little parmesan cheese. Bake half an hour or until fork tender, in 350 oven.

BREAST OF CHICKEN WITH LEMON JUICE

There are so many ways of cooking that delectable breast. This way of doing it insures a moist and tender "fried chicken".

Rinse piece of chicken off with cold water and dry it on a paper towel. Place on plate and drench with lemon juice. (Rub a halved lemon all over it.) Put this in the refrigerator and let it stand for 10 minutes.

Cream a little salt, ground pepper and 1/8 tsp. powdered marjoram with a tbsp. of very soft butter; rub this all over your cold chicken and sprinkle with a little paprika.

Place on a piece of heavy foil (buttered). Draw up the sides but do not cover entirely. This may be placed on a foil pie tin and baked in 350 oven for forty minutes, or so, until fork tender.

The old fashioned way of shaking pieces of chicken in a paper bag with salt, pepper, paprika and flour and fried in butter or cooking oil is hard to beat.

CHINESE CHICKEN

This recipe was given to me by a friend who had lived in China for many years.

½ small broiler; 1 tbsp. butter; ½ c. fresh or frozen mushrooms; ½ c. hot water; 1 small piece of fresh ginger (finely chopped); ¼ c. soya sauce; speck of pepper.

Joint the chicken, wash and dry on paper towel. Saute in butter until pale yellow, add the mushrooms, (sliced), soya sauce, and ginger; simmer for a minute or two and pour the hot water over all. No salt or extra seasoning required. Candied ginger, two teaspoons chopped or 1 teaspoon powdered ginger may be substituted for fresh ginger. This should be covered and simmered until chicken is fork tender. Instant rice may be served with this. Bottled chutney, as a relish.

MARINATED CHICKEN

1 chicken breast; 2 tbsp. french or Italian dressing; fine bread crumbs, or commercial chicken stuffing; seasoning, salt and pepper; minced parsley.

Marinate chicken in salad dressing and let it stand for an hour or so. Roll in seasoned crumbs or stuffing and fry in a tablespoon of butter, turning, and when nicely browned on both sides, partly cover with foil and let cook until tender. Remaining marinade may be poured over it before covering.

CHICKEN A LA KING

Of all ways of doing chicken, this one has been the most abused — usually made of sad, left-over chicken, white sauce (paper hangers paste, style) and all sorts of awful additions — green peas, canned pimento, green pepper, etc., etc.

My recipe came originally from a famous restaurant in New York and the big secret is, that it is made of *freshly* cooked hot chicken. This has been adjusted to make one generous serving and is a delectable and delicate dish. It may be served on a very thin slice of buttered toast or in a patty shell. Frozen patty shells in packages of 6 can be baked according to directions and kept indefinitely in a covered tin, or you may buy one or two at your pet baker's .

1 med. chicken breast or ½ sm. fryer; 2 fresh mushrooms (med.); 1 sm. green onion; 1 tsp. finely cut fresh parsley; 1 tbsp. butter; 1 tsp. salt; 1/8 tsp. ground pepper; 1/8 tsp. accent; 4 blanched almonds (split); 1 egg yolk; 1 des. spoon sherry; ½ c. top milk or "creamy" ½ c. chicken stock; season to taste.

Method:

Place butter, salt and pepper in small heavy skillet or sauce-pan and heat.

Wash and skin chicken and joint (if small fryer used). Saute lightly for 10 minutes. Add 1 cup boiling water, cover tightly and simmer until tender. Remove chicken from bones, cut into 1" pieces and keep hot until you make the following sauce.

Sauce for Chicken a la King

Melt 1 tbsp. butter and saute the thinly sliced, peeled mushrooms for *not* more than a minute (do not brown and shrivel). Blend in 1 tbsp. flour, ¼ tsp. salt and add ½ c. rich milk or "half and half" cream. Stir until it thickens, adding ½ c. of the hot liquid chicken was cooked in. Add beaten yolk of egg and the sherry. Season with a little more salt and pepper, if necessary and let come to a low boil. Add the chicken which has been kept hot. Stir and heat well.

Add the raw, finely sliced green onion and snipped parsley. Serve on buttered thin toast, or heated up pre-baked patty shell. Split almonds are optional and may be sprinkled on top.

V

Eggs, Omelettes
and Souffles

The refuge for all ages from one year to 100 and the quickest and easiest to prepare.

Eggs are high in food values, minerals, proteins and vitamins. They can be cooked in hundreds of different ways or eaten raw in an Egg-Nog (with a little whiskey or brandy of course).

THE BOILED EGG

Coddling is preferable to boiling and insures a firm tender egg. Have a quart sauce-pan full of *boiling water*. Rinse eggs in hot water from the tap to prevent cracking and slip into the boiling water. Cover pot and *remove* from heat. If you like a *three minute boiled egg* let it stand in the pot of hot water for six minutes. If you prefer it a little firmer leave it for another minute or so.

HARD BOILED EGGS

If you are doing four or more eggs, use more water and a larger pot. Cover and let stand off the heat as above and leave them for a half an hour at least. Plunge cooked eggs in cold water, prick end of shell to prevent discoloration and when cool store in refrigerator until needed.

OMELETTES

Having just read two books devoted entirely to the subject of "How to make a perfect omelette" and suffered many sad and stringy failures, I am picking out the salient points and leaving it up to you.

One delightful French woman tells us that "Omelettes are made with love and delicacy and a soupcon of patience."

"The best way to ruin an omelette or scrambled eggs is to *over-cook*, making a tough, stringy dish, and not welcome to the palate."

It does not take more than a minute to make a plain omelette and no more than two or three if ingredients to make a filling are added.

French cooks keep their omelette pans exclusively for the making of omelettes and those made with a fishy filling have a separate one.

Those pans must *never* be washed, but merely wiped with a soft cloth or paper towel. They acquire a soft, oily, but never greasy surface which is most unlikely to stick.

A mechanical egg beater is outrageous! *Never*, never use anything but an ordinary fork.

WATER FOR A FRENCH OMELETTE

In making any kind of omelette, plain, filled or sweet, always use water — *never* milk or cream.

The most important rule of all in making a filled omelette is to saute whatever you are using in the warming butter and pour the egg mixture on top. You are thus insured of a hot filling in the middle of your omelette. This is a direct reversal of the ordinary way of making this light and delicate dish. After many, many trials and tough stringy productions had almost decided to go back to old "scrambled eggs", when I discovered that the principal solution of all my troubles was in the heat of the pan. Heat your pan slowly, put the required amount of butter in and raise the heat until it is pale brown — and the pan is quite hot. Pour in your egg mixture and lift off heat for a few seconds, shaking the pan and drawing the mixture from sides of pan to centre, allowing liquid to form an envelope, before putting back on heat and completing. This all takes but a few more seconds and you will be able to fold omelette by lifting the edge nearest you and rolling over on to your very hot plate.

PLAIN OMELETTE — FRENCH WAY

1 dessert spoon butter; 2 eggs;
2 tbsp. water; salt and pepper to taste.

The way the eggs are beaten for any omelette is most important. They should be beaten with a fork for twenty to thirty seconds only, as over beating makes the eggs watery. Add seasonings, and 2 *scant* tablespoons of water.

Place omelette pan over low heat until it has warmed up, add butter, turn heat up and when it is light brown, add beaten egg mixture. Lift pan off heat for a moment and start pulling eggs in to centre of pan, letting the liquid run to sides — put back on heat and when envelope is formed, keep on drawing eggs to centre until creamy and cooked. Roll omelette off on to a piping hot plate and eat it at once.

FILLED OMELETTES

The French chefs make hundreds of different varieties of "filled" omelettes. They all have impressive names but, with the exception of a few raw ingredients, are inevitably made in the same way. This is a direct reversal from our way. Most recipes tell you to pour the eggs into pan and when they are a little coagulated, pour in the fillings. The French way is to add *filling* to the hot butter in pan, sauteing for a moment or two to heat and *then* pouring the egg mixture on top. When the omelette is folded, the filling will be in the *middle*.

There are a few exceptions to this. Snipped bacon, raw liver, or anything raw should be cooked in a separate pan and then added *first* in making the omelette.

There seems to be no limit in using any kind of scraps or left overs by following this procedure. I have tried this with various bits and pieces — asparagus, chicken, cooked vegetables, etc. The omelette turns over with a nice hot inside, instead of clammy cool bits scattered through it.

CHEESE OMELETTE

2 eggs, lightly beaten; 1 tbsp. water; salt and pepper;
1 dessert spoon butter; 2 tbsp. any kind grated cheese.

Add the cheese to the egg mixture and pour into the hot butter. Increase heat and pull eggs in from sides, completing as usual.

TOMATO OMELETTE

I tbsp. butter; 2 eggs;
1 tbsp. water; salt and pepper; 1 small ripe tomato

Beat eggs lightly, add water. In omelette pan, saute the peeled slices of tomato, season with salt and pepper — (It just needs to be heated) — Pour the eggs on top and complete as in plain omelette.

TOMATO AND CHEESE OMELETTE

2 or 3 slices raw tomato; 2 eggs; 1 tbsp. water;
add: 1 tbsp. grated parmesan cheese;
1 dessert spoon butter and seasoning.

Saute the tomato slices in warming butter until just hot — (do not let it get mushy or it may stick). With pan quite hot, add cheese to regulation mix and pour over the sauted tomatoes. Complete according to directions.

FRESH MUSHROOM OMELETTE

½ c. sliced mushrooms; 2 eggs;
1 tbsp. cold water; 1 dessert spoon butter.

Heat pan slowly, add butter and when melted, saute the sliced mushrooms until lightly browned, add egg mixture made according to basic omelette and proceed in the same way. Season with salt and pepper just before you fold.

All filled omelettes are made in the same way, sauteing the filling *before* adding eggs.

LEFT OVER ANYTHING

Follow procedure for filled omelette — warming bits and pieces of cooked food or vegetables before adding regulation egg mix.

It is not advisable to make a large omelette.

Plain poached eggs are rather invalidish and dull, but can be made quite gourmet and appetizing by using milk, consomme, tomato juice, etc. and can be done in your smallest skillet. This is a very easy way, remembering that eggs in any form must be cooked slowly.

Heat whatever liquid you choose, to boiling point. Drop one egg in carefully and cover. *Remove* from heat and let stand until set. Snipped parsley, grated cheese and paprika and a little salt sprinkled on top and served on a slice of very thin, buttered toast. Add liquid.

BAKED EGGS — SPANISH MAYBE?

1 or 2 eggs; 1 tbsp. butter;
1 tbsp. chili sauce; fine crumbs.

Use butter to grease a small casserole. Place eggs in and cover with the chili sauce, sprinkle with fine dry bread crumbs and bake very slowly until set.

BAKED EGGS WITH MUSTARD

Use small casserole — well buttered. Place eggs in and smear with little daubs of made mustard. Season with salt and bake until set. This can be done on top of stove in small pan, covered and very slow heat.

SCRAMBLED EGGS

2 eggs; 2 tbsp. water;
salt and pepper; 2 tsp. butter.

Melt butter in small frying pan. Beat the eggs lightly as in the French way. Add water and pour mixture into your medium hot pan. Cook slowly, stirring until thick and creamy. Finely cut parsley may be added.

SCRAMBLED EGGS No. 2

Water in proportion to one scant tablespoon to one egg makes a much better scramble than milk or cream. The same procedure for fillings can be followed as for the French way of making omelettes. Heating the filling, whatever it is, in the butter, adding the eggs and mixing and cooking it very slowly. It should be creamy and delicious. In making any omelette or scrambled eggs, always add the grated cheese required to the beaten egg and water mixture. (1 tbsp. grated cheese)

POACHED EGGS AND GRATED CHEESE

Poach two eggs in whatever liquid you choose. Sprinkle a tablespoon of grated cheese on top and cover for a minute or two until cheese melts. Lift out carefully and place on a very thin piece of buttered toast. Season with salt and pepper.

ONION POACH

½ c. milk; salt and pepper; 1 sm. onion, sliced very thinly; 2 sm. eggs or 1 large one.

In small pan, cook thin onions in milk until tender. Season and slip the eggs in. Cover and let stand on "simmer" until eggs are set.

Lightly butter 2 thin slices of toast, put eggs on top, pour onions and liquid on top.

CURRIED EGGS

1 c. delicate cream sauce; ½ tsp. good curry powder; salt and pepper to taste; 1 tsp. finely cut parsley; 1 tsp. lemon juice; dash of garlic powder, if liked.

Mix all together and bring to a boil and slice in one or two hard boiled eggs. (Boil the eggs according to recipe and make your sauce while they are quietly and tenderly cooking).

SOUFFLÉS

In making any kind or size of a souffle, if the following rule is observed, you will find the chances of a fallen, soggy souffle greatly reduced.

When you have your cream cheese sauce completed and the whites of eggs well beaten and ready to fold in, take a tablespoon of the beaten *whites* and beat it into the cooled cheese mixture *before* folding the balance carefully in. Spoon it into buttered mould, or casserole and bake in moderate oven, 325, until puffed up and light brown. — Thirty five to forty minutes. Test with straw. Serve at once.

CHEESE SOUFFLÉ

1 tbsp. flour; 1 tbsp. butter — level; ½ tsp. salt; speck of cayenne; ½ c. milk; ¼ c. grated cheese; 1 egg, separated.

In small pan make a rich cream sauce by melting butter, blending in flour, salt and cayenne. Add milk, stir and cook until thick. Cool — add cheese and egg yolk. Beat well and let it get quite cold. Beat white of egg until stiff and follow as in above procedure.

PICKLED EGGS

6 hard boiled eggs (shelled); 1 c. seasoned vinegar; ¼ c. water; a few cloves; bit of dried ginger; 1 tsp. salt; 1 tsp. onion powder; 1 tsp. whole tiny red peppers; 1 clove of fresh garlic (optional).

Bring vinegar, water, and all seasonings to a boil and simmer for two or three minutes. Place eggs in wide mouthed jar and pour the vinegar over them. Let stand for several hours. Remove eggs and strain the vinegar. Put the eggs back in jar and cover with the strained vinegar. More flavored vinegar may be added to cover eggs completely. These eggs will keep (in refrigerator) for two or three months. Keep well covered.

May be used for garnish, sliced, halved, or chopped and added to any salad containing meat.

STUFFED EGGS

There are dozens of ways of making stuffed eggs interesting.
Cut hard boiled eggs in two (lengthwise).
Mash yolks and season with salt, pepper and a little soft butter. With this foundation, try various additions, such as:

1. *Finely chopped celery*
2. *A teaspoon anchovy paste or 1 smoked anchovy*
3. *1 tsp. flavored vinegar and capers*
   1 tbsp. chopped ripe olives
4. *1 tsp. prepared horseradish*
5. *Chopped parsley and grated onion*
6. *Slivered, blanched almonds and curry*
   and anything you happen to think of.

Add the mixture back into the halves and sprinkle with paprika and a little finely cut parsley. Judge quantities of anything add to the number of eggs you are doing. I use a little nasturtium or papaya vinegar, or any flavored vinegar in any of these.

Halved or thick slices of hard boiled eggs are much more attractive if sprinkled with a good dash or any "seasoning salt"; my favourite is "Johnny's Salad Elegance".

VI

Meats,
Curries and Stews

Buying meat in small quantities may seem difficult to you at first.

There are literally hundreds of ways of cooking a hot meat dinner for one. It is only a matter of choice and capacity.

If you plan your dinners for a week and on your semi-weekly shopping binges purchase exactly what you need according to your appetite you will save yourself endless worry and waste.

Lamb, veal, pork chops; take your choice, ground round or shoulder is preferable to hamburger; less fat and scrappy bits. Freshly sliced bacon is better than packaged; your butcher will gladly do it for you as thick or thin and lean as you like. The odd meal of bacon and eggs and vegetables or salad is not to be sneezed at.

Sweet breads if you can get them fresh and calves liver are both delicate luxuries.

We must not forget the good old stew meat, lamb or beef and the nice little pot roast, (all these can be done on top of the stove, covered of course).

HAMBURGER

Hamburger — that most versatile of all meats, lends itself agreeably to cooking for one.

Ground round or shoulder is preferable. It has much less fat and is made of the best meat. Do not have patties thin and over-cooked or they will be dry and tasteless. This is my favourite method and I call it:

LAZY STEAK

¼ lb. ground meat - shoulder or round; ¼ tsp. salt; 1/8 tsp. freshly gr. pepper; 2 or 3 drops worcester sauce; 2 tabls. "creamy" or top milk; 2 tsp. lemon juice; dash of "Accent".

Mix seasonings with the "creamy" or top milk. Put ground meat on a piece of wax paper and with a fork crush the seasoned mixture into it. Form into an inch and a half thick patty. Sprinkle both sides with the lemon juice and prick in with fork. Have heavy iron skillet piping hot: brush it over with a little fat and brown the steak quickly on both sides and just let it cook until it is a nice pale pink inside. Put it out on a hot plate, add a bit of butter and any juice from pan. (You may add a little hot water to pan and boil almost dry).

This makes a deliciously tender steak.

ELEGANT SHEPHERD'S PIE

¼ lb. ground shoulder; 1 small onion or two green ones thinly sliced; ¼ c. chopped celery; ¼ tsp. dry mustard; ½ tsp. salt; ½ tin consomme; a little ground pepper, to taste; 1 tsp. Kitchen Bouquet.

Brown meat well — stirring to separate it. Add the soup and all seasonings. Simmer with the added onion and celery for ten minutes or so. If it needs thickening sprinkle with a little flour and stir it until it is just right for potato topping.

Prepare "Instant Mashed Potatoes" according to directions. Transfer the hot meat mixture to buttered casserole and heap the potato on top. Sprinkle on a little finely chopped parsley and paprika to make it look pretty and serve it at once. It you care to put it in the oven for a minute to brown a bit, you may like it better, but this way is a quick "top stove" method and is delicious.

GOURMET MEAT PATTIES

To finish up the gound meat saga, have this Gourmet Meat Ball thing some night when you think you have completely lost your appetite.

¼ lb. ground round; ½ tsp. salt, ¼ c. chopped fresh mushrooms; 2 green onions, thinly sliced; 1/8 tsp. ground pepper; ¼ tsp. celery salt; a little Accent; 1 tbsp. fine bread crumbs; 2 tbsps. evaporated milk.

Place the meat on a piece of waxed paper and with a fork blend in all the other ingredients. Make into two little patties, roll them in two tablespoons finely chopped parsley and fry in a little butter until they are nice and crisply brown on both sides. Now, lower the heat and cover each patty with a teaspoon of sour cream or yogurt and put a lid on pan and just let it get hot.

Add a dash of paprika to each serving. These are nice with stewed tomatoes.

It sounds like a lot of meat but is not more than the gourmet steak and you will eat it all.

PORK PARCEL DINNER

One pork chop; 1 thinly sliced onion;
1 thickly sliced raw potato; salt and pepper.

Cut most of the fat off the chop and brown slightly. Place it on a good sized square of heavy foil. Put the onion slices on, season, and pile the thickly sliced potatoes on top, add more seasoning. Now draw up all sides of foil into a "drugstore" wrapped parcel. Have it well sealed, but not too tight.

Place parcel in a pan and bake for one hour in a 300 oven. You might put two or three apples in at the same time. This makes a complete dinner.

SPARE RIBS

These should be parboiled for twenty minutes, seasoned, barbecue sauce sprinkled and baked or broiled until tender.

PORK TENDERLOIN

This, an economical dinner for one, can be frenched by your butcher and fried in a little butter, seasoned to your taste and served with instant mashed potatoes, etc.

HUNGARIAN VEAL CUTLET

Brown meat in heavy skillet and add: 1 small onion; 1 stalk celery; ½ carrot; ½ potato.

All sliced rather thickly, season with salt, pepper and a half teaspoon of paprika. Pile all this on top of chop and cover with boiling water. When it has come to a boil, turn heat to "simmer" and let it cook slowly until fork tender. Keep it covered and a few minutes before serving, add a tablespoon of sour cream. Just let it heat and not boil. Chopped parsley may be sprinkled on top and a sprinkle of paprika.

This makes an attractive "plate meal".

VEAL BIRD

1 portion of thin fillet of veal;
½ c. of parsley stuffing.

Roll up and tie with string.

Brown in a little butter and bake until tender. 1 tablespoon finely chopped parsley added to ordinary chicken stuffing — grated lemon rind is an improvement.

INDIAN CURRY

A real Indian curry is always made with fresh uncooked meat — pork, mutton, lamb or beef. It is not a mere matter of stirring a little "any old kind" of curry powder into a stew.

The meat should be cut in small squares and fried in butter with the following ingredients: salt, curry powder, chopped onion, and celery, lemon, or lime juice. This recipe has been adapted for two servings as it is delicious the third day — or can be frozen.

1 tbsp. fat, cooking oil, or butter; 1 med. onion, chopped; ½ c. celery and some tops, chopped; 1 dessert spoon or more if you like, curry; ½ tsp. salt; 2 tbsps. lemon or lime juice; 1 lb. uncooked meat cut in inch pieces; ½ c. milk; boiling water.

In heavy skillet fry the onion, celery, salt and meat until brown, add the curry powder, mixed with milk — fry for another ten minutes, add the lemon or lime juice and a little water if it is very thick. Cover pan tightly and just let it simmer for an hour or so. Raisins, peeled raw apple, cut in chunks, or banana may be added if desired.

The best curry to use is "VENCATACHELLUM", quite a mouthful, eh!

QUICK CURRY

Ground round or shoulder can be used in many ways for one person.

If you use the kind of hamburger that has a lot of fat in it do it this way.

¼ lb. ground meat; ½ c. chopped onion; ¼ c. finely minced celery; ½ c. chopped peeled apple; ½ tin consomme; ½ tsp. salt; 1 tsp. curry, more if you like; ½ c. sherry; 1 tsp. Kitchen Bouquet.

Fry the meat and onions until light brown, add the celery, consomme and curry, salt and pepper. Let this come to a boil and add the chopped apples. Simmer, stirring occasionally until apples are cooked. Sprinkle with a little flour on top if you think it needs thickening and add at the last the sherry or any red wine that you happen to have.

Serve with rice (Instant, if you do not want to bother boiling regular long grain rice). Of course, you will have Indian Chutney with this. A little goes a long way.

LIVER DELICIOUS

Fresh calf's liver is an expensive luxury, but it is high in vitamins and a slice occasionally won't ruin one.

This recipe was sent to a famous columnist on the "Victoria Times" who happened to mention that he disliked liver. I usually fry my slice of liver quickly in a little butter, but this method is called "Liver Delicious" and is broiled.

1 slice liver, at least ½" thick; 2 tsp. butter; 2 tsp. lemon juice; ¼ tsp. crumbled oregano; ¼ tsp. salt and a little ground pepper.

Cream butter with lemon juice, add seasonings. Place liver on a piece of foil on flat pan and coat the top with half of mixture. Place in a cold broiler five inches from heat and broil four minutes. Turn it over and coat the other side and broil four minutes more. Take it out, sprinkle with a little finely chopped parsley and any juice in the foil. Have your plate piping hot and serve with instant mashed potatoes and frenched green beans.

CARBONNADE DE BOEUF

1 lb. beef chuck cut in 1½" cubes; 2½ tbsp. butter; 2 tbsp. flour; ¼ tsp. fresh thyme leaves (dried will do); 1 small bit of bay leaf; 1 dessert spoon, flavored vinegar (Papaya); 1 c. beer; 1 tbsp. chopped parsley; 2 slices medium onion; 1 tsp. sugar; ½ tsp. salt; 1/8 tsp. freshly gound pepper.

Dredge beef well with half the flour and sear in half the butter. Brown it well. Add parsley, thyme, bay leaf, salt, pepper, vinegar and beer enough to cover (if one cup is not enough, add more).

Bring all this to a boil, reduce heat and simmer for one hour (add more beer if necessary). *Saute* onion slices in other half butter, add the sugar and cook until onions are slightly glazed. Put this with the simmering meat mixture and cook fifteen minutes more or until meat is tender. May be heated in a day or two, it makes two good portions.

BEEF STEW

Do not use left-over roast meat in a stew. It will be certain to be tough and stringy. The only way to use pre-cooked meats is to make a mince or a "Humble Shepherd's Pie", and use any left over gravy, etc.

Every woman has her own way of making a stew. This is the way I make mine. I always make enough for three meals, and by freezing one part of it for later use, keeping part over a couple of days to mature and improve, avoid a repetition.

1½ lbs. shoulder or lean brisket.

Cut in small pieces. Brown well in heavy skillet and add seasonings. Cover with boiling water and let it simmer for an hour or more until nearly cooked. I then add just enough vegetables for my first hot meal. One small carrot, one onion and one potato cut in two and a few pieces of celery. Cook until they are firm but not mushy. Fish them out and divide stew into two remaining parts.

Cook vegetables separately when you warm up the frozen portion. Your stew will be much nicer.

QUICKIE STEW WITH INSTANT DUMPLINGS

1 small can of beef stew; Dumplings made of any good prepared biscuit mix, using
½ cup biscuit mix; 1/3rd cup milk.

Heat stew to boiling in a small pot, with a good tight fitting lid. It may be very thick and require ¼ cup tomato juice or hot water. When gently bubbling add the dumplings in tablespoons, (should make three).

Cook *uncovered* over low heat for ten minutes. *Cover tightly* and cook for ten minutes longer. This to me is an unusual way of cooking dumplings but it is according to directions on box and they are beautifully light and fluffy.

These dumplings may be added to chicken fricassee. Place on top of meat and do not allow to sink in the liquid or they become soggy.

STEAK

Beef tenderloin is really the most economical way of having a broiled steak for one, as it can be done in a heavy skillet on top of the stove with a minimum of smoke. Here are two ways that I do it.

Have your small heavy pan sizzling hot, brush lightly with a bit of fat. Turn on your fan, open the windows and place thick little steak on smoking skillet, leave it one minute, turn and lower heat, cook for two minutes and turn again, cook for two more minutes. This is for medium rare — you would not dream of ruining that delicious and expensive steak by cooking it well done — would you?

Put steak on a very hot plate with a small piece of butter, salt and pepper to taste.

NEW METHOD BROILED STEAK

I saw this in a magazine and hesitated for a long time before trying it. Heat skillet as above recipe calls for and sprinkle a good teaspoon or more of salt on dry pan. Place steak on top of salt and cook for two minutes, turn and cook another two minutes. The meat will not stick and the pan will be quite dry. Steak is not a bit too salty and there is also much less smoke. Be brave and try it.

CREOLE ROUND STEAK

1 piece of thick steak (for one); ¼ c. tomato catsup; ¼ c. hot water; 1 tbsp. onion soup mix (shaken); 1 tbsp. fat, bacon grease or butter.

In a small heavy bottomed sauce pan, brown the piece of meat well on both sides. Combine the catsup, water and soup mix and pour over the meat. Reduce heat to simmer, cover tightly and let it cook gently for about an hour — try it with a fork. You may make a little gravy by adding a sprinkle of flour to what is left in the pan and stir with more water added if necessary. This should be cooked in oven ordinarily, but if you are not baking anything else and do not want to heat large oven for a very small dish, it will cook very well on top if done slowly and kept tightly covered.

Easy Baked Ham

1 large can baked ham

20 cloves

1½ tablespoons brown sugar, maple syrup or honey.

½ cup orange juice

Stick cloves into top and sides of ham, spread mustard on top, then brown sugar, maple syrup or
Pour orange juice into baking pan, add ham
bake in 350 oven for 1 hour.

CORN BEEF HASH

For a cold night "Quickie" this is easily made even if you are a bit late getting in.

1 half small tin of corned beef; 1 cup of potato slices;
a little salt, pepper and dry mustard.

Peel a medium sized potato, cut in thick slices and parboil until almost cooked, *Chop* corned beef and potato pieces with all the seasonings. *Add* two finely minced green onions, 1 tablespoon cream (evaporated is nice), mix well and form into one large flat cake. Fry in butter until nicely browned on both sides.

If you are really hungry place a poached egg on top and sprinkle with a little hot chili sauce or tomato catsup.

Please don't make this with a sad cold boiled potato left from yesterday.

VII

Vegetables

We should take advantage of all the fresh vegetables and fruits we possibly can. One should have no compunction in cooking the exact amount required for one dinner. Warmed over vegetables are not appetizing.

In using any of the frozen vegetables, take out the portion you can eat and tie up the bag and replace in freezer. When you buy frozen packages of peas, etc., rattle them to see if they are separated and not refrozen in a solid block.

Note: Half a package may be cut in two and remainder placed in a baggie and put back in freezer.

POTATOES

There are many ways of cooking potatoes. When having a complete dinner cooked in the oven it is wise to have the good old

BAKED POTATO

Speed up baking time by par boiling for five minutes. Prick to avoid bursting in that nice clean oven and bake until tender.

PRETEND SCALLOPED POTATOES

1 middle sized potato — ¼" slices;
1 middle sized onion, thinly sliced; butter, pepper, salt, Accent.

Place alternately with seasonings and bits of butter in between on a good square of heavy foil. Bring up the sides into a neat parcel, sealed with a "drugstore" wrap and put parcel on a foil pieplate. Bake in 350 oven thirty or forty minutes.

Very nice with cold meat.

PRETEND FRENCH FRIED POTATOES

Cut a peeled potato into oblong pieces, the same as for French Fry. Soak in cold water for a few minutes and dry on a paper towel. Scatter them on a buttered pie tin or any flat pan, using no more than one teaspoon butter. Turn to butter both sides and see that they are apart.

Bake in 375 oven about fifteen minutes. (May be done in Toast-R-Oven). They should be crisp and light brown and will be if you use as little butter as possible and place in hot pan. *Do not* add salt until served.

QUICK CREAMED POTATOES

1 medium potato (according to appetite); 1 dessert spoon butter; 1 dessert flour; salt and pepper; 2/3 c. milk.

Peel potatoes and cut in 1 inch blocks. Cook in boiling water until almost tender, but not mushy, drain all but ¼ cup water. Add seasonings and butter. Stir for a minute and sprinkle on flour before adding the milk. Stir gently to avoid breaking up potato cubes and cook until it comes to a boil. Celery salt, garlic powder and a dash of Accent may be added with milk. Chopped parsley lends enchantment.

QUICK PAN BROILED POTATOES

Scrub a fairly large potato and grate on medium grater. I use an eight inch skillet for this method. Grease it well with bacon grease or butter. Spread grated potatoes to the depth of ¼ inch. Cover pan and cook over medium heat until the bottom is brown. Turn it over and cook until brown on other side. Season with salt and serve at once. A little grated onion may be added to potato if desired.

ASPARAGUS

When cooking asparagus, you will find a middle sized, deep bread pan very useful. Crumple some foil and place at one end of pan so that the heads are out of the water. Pour boiling water to the depth of two or three inches, season with salt and Accent and boil until the stocks are just tender. Do not over-cook. The tops will steam and be firm and just right.

BAKED BEANS

You can pretend you are having old fashioned baked beans this way:

1 can pork and beans; ½ tsp. salt; 1 thick slice bacon in inch pieces and par-boiled 5 min.; 1 des. spoon molasses; ½ tsp. mustard; ½ c. boiling water.

Place in small deep casserole and bake for about an hour in 300 oven.

BAKED BEETS

1 c thinly sliced raw, peeled beets; 1 tbsp. butter; ¼ tsp. salt; 1 tsp. sugar; ¼ c. boiling water; 1/8 tsp. freshly ground pepper.

Place beets in small buttered casserole. Add the seasonings and boiling water. Dot the butter over beets and bake (closely covered with foil) until tender. May be done with other baking things in 350 oven, but require only 30 min.

BROCCOLI

This expensive vegetable with its weight mostly in the stalk can be made to do twice. Buy exactly what you want for one meal, cut the tops off, leaving about an inch of stem. Cook in an inch of boiling water until just tender.

The stalks can be cut slantwise very thinly and cooked in boiling salted water for another dinner. You know, of course, that Broccoli must be soaked in cold water with a little salt to draw out any visiting insects and remove sand, etc. Cook heads of broccoli 5 minutes stem end down in an inch or two of boiling water. Do not over-cook.

DIGESTIBLE CABBAGE

A portion of cabbage, (your size), salt and a piping hot heavy skillet with about a cup of boiling salted water.

Shave cabbage as thinly as you can. Pop into rapidly boiling water and cook uncovered for only three or four minutes, or until crisply tender.

Drain, add a little butter, pepper and salt and 1 teaspoon vinegar or lemon juice.

BAKED CARROTS

1 dessert spoon butter; 1 c. peeled shredded carrots; ¼ tsp. salt, pepper; ¼ tsp. sugar; 2 green onions, sliced thinly; ¼ cup (or a little more) water.

Put all ingredients in a small buttered casserole, covering with the hot water. Cover the dish with foil and bake in 350 oven until they are tender.

Vegetables should be cooked quickly and crisply, in as little water as possible, otherwise, they will become waterlogged and mushy. The water from celery, carrots and asparagus should be poured off and kept for diluting that half tin of soup, or making a home-made cream soup or sauce.

CORN

Cook a lone ear of corn in a small bread pan, well covered with boiling water and add a teaspoon of sugar. No salt until cooked and buttered.

Keep an oblong of heavy foil for covering bread tin cooking — It can be fitted over and used many times.

TOMATO SLICES

1 good sized tomato, cut 3/4 inch slices;
season with salt, pepper, and sugar; dip in cornmeal, both sides.
Saute lightly in melted butter until light brown.

FRIED TOMATOES

3 thick slices firm ripe tomatoes; 1 tbsp. flour; ½ tsp. salt;
little freshly ground pepper; pinch of gr. basil; 1 tbsp. butter;
¼ c. light cream.
Dip tomato slices in mixture of flour, salt and pepper and basil. Heat butter in heavy skillet. Add tomato slices and cook slowly until golden brown on both sides. Remove with spatula to hot plate. Stir cream into butter left in hot pan. Heat well and spoon over tomatoes.

CORNMEAL FRIED TOMATOES

Cut in thick slices.
Sprinkle with salt, pepper and a speck of powdered basil.
Dip in cornmeal (both sides).
Fry in bacon grease or butter until crisp and light brown.
For quantity — do these as capacity or appetite demands.

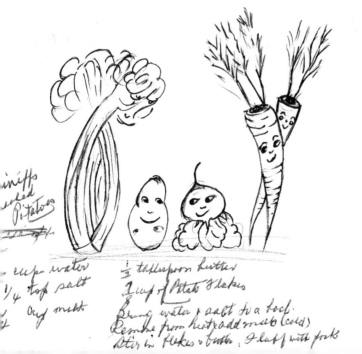

cup water
¼ tsp salt

½ tablespoon butter
1 cup of Potato Flakes
Bring water & salt to a boil.
Remove from heat add milk (cold)
Stir in flakes & butter. Fluff with forks

VIII

Entrees, Cheesies and Pancakes

BAKED BREAD AND CHEESE CUSTARD

2 thin slices of bread; butter; 1/3 c. coarsely grated old cheese; salt, pepper and ¼ tsp. dry mustard; 1 small egg; 1 c. milk.

Cut crusts of bread and butter one side. Place one slice, buttered side down, in small 5" casserole, scatter a little more than half the cheese on and add the other slice of bread, buttered side up. Beat egg thoroughly, add the salt, pepper, mustard and milk. Pour over the bread cheese mixture. Let stand for about half an hour or until it becomes soaked. Scatter the rest of the cheese on top and sprinkle with a little paprika.

Bake in 300 oven 40 minutes until it becomes light brown.

STEAMED CHEESE CUSTARD

This is a delicate and nourishing dish and, as my Irish father used to say, "Fit for a lady in her confinement."

1 c. milk; 1 large egg; ¼ c. old cheese, grated; ¼ tsp. salt; speck of cayenne; 2 drops worcester sauce.

In small saucepan melt the cheese with half the milk, add the rest of the milk gradually, but do not let it get more than moderately hot. Let cool a little and add beaten egg and seasonings. Mix well and pour into a small buttered casserole or two little pyrex custard cups. Place these in pan (a bun warmer with tight cover is excellent), cover with a piece of foil and pour boiling water around dish until it is within an inch of top. (Put a little slightly rumpled foil under cups to keep them off direct heat). Put the lid on and steam on *low heat* for 20 minutes, until set, (try with a knife). Too high heat will curdle and ruin custard. They should be smooth as satin. Are equally nice cold or can be warmed up next day.

DELICATE CHEESE CUSTARD

1 tbsp. Imperial creamed cheese (old); ¾ c. milk; ¼ tsp. salt; speck of pepper; 1 egg; 1/8 tsp. dry mustard (Coleman's).

Blend and melt cheese, milk and seasonings in small pan until it is creamy. Cool a little and add well beaten egg. Heat well and put in a buttered custard cup or small deep casserole, cover with a bit of foil. Place in a saucepan on a piece of slightly crumpled foil and pour boiling water around it, half way up side of cup. Cover tin and let *simmer* only and steam until set and firm.

Do not let water boil hard as it curdles custard. It should be very smooth and is delicious. It is good hot or cold and may be warmed up in hot water.

OLD FASHIONED WELSH RAREBIT

2 tsp. butter; 1 tsp. cornstarch or flour; salt and cayenne pepper to taste; 1/8 tsp. worcester sauce; 1/3 c. coarsely grated old cheese; ½ c. milk or preferably BEER.

Melt butter, add cornstarch and stir until it bubbles, add milk or beer gradually, cook a minute or so and add the cheese; stir until cheese melts and it is creamy.

Serve at once on a piece of thin buttered toast.

PANCAKES — *"All kinds of Pancakes"*

If you are in the habit of using any of the excellent pancake mixes (specially the ones with buttermilk) do not read this chapter as it deals with only ancient and honorable methods of making feather-light, digestible and inexpensive pancakes.

BREAD CRUMB PANCAKES

½ cup warm milk; 1 tbsp. butter; ½ tsp. salt; 1 tsp. sugar; ½ cup soft white bread crumbs; 1 egg; ¼ cup flour; 1 tsp. b. powder.

Warm milk with butter, sugar and salt and pour over bread crumbs; allow this to cool — *beat in 1 egg*, add flour and baking powder, beat well and cook in the usual way on a greased griddle, turning when bubbles form; these are at their best with butter and maple sugar or syrup but are nice with white sugar and lemon juice.

POTATO PANCAKES

Make as above, omitting sugar and adding ½ cup grated raw potato: Peel one potato and soak in cold water for ½ hour, dry and grate.

These are very good with apple sauce.

YEAST PANCAKES

These pancakes are particularly light and tender but have to be started about an hour ahead of when you intend to eat them.

½ package of dry yeast (is 1 tsp.); ¼ cup warm water; 1 tsp. sugar;
Let stand until it rises (about ten minutes).
Place following ingredients in a quart sized bowl.

1 well beaten egg; ½ cup warm milk (lukewarm);
¾ cup bread flour; ¼ tsp. salt; 1 tbsp. cooking oil;
beat well and add dissolved yeast.

Cover bowl with a damp cloth and let stand until well risen and bubbly (it may take an hour). Do not beat this down but spoon out on hot buttered griddle and cook as usual.

APPLE PANCAKES

½ cup soft white bread crumbs; ¾ cup hot milk; 1 tblsp. butter.
Pour hot milk over crumbs and butter and let cool.

Add:

1 beaten egg; ¼ tsp. salt; ½ grated raw apple or half a cup; 1 tsp. sugar; ¼ cup bread flour; 1 tsp. baking powder.

These are nice with pork tenderloin or a couple of pork chops or with maple syrup and butter as usual.

If a big fat John is making these he will probably eat them all but if any batter is left over cover it and keep in refrig. until next day.

Cook these as usual in a heavy frying pan turning when bubbles form. Serve very hot.

VERY DARING PANCAKES

Follow above recipe and add one tablespoon parmesan cheese (packaged) or 1 tablespoon grated old "Rat".

JANE'S SCOTCH TEA PANCAKES. (Best)

¼ cup butter; ½ cup icing sugar; 1 egg (beaten); 1 cup sifted flour; 2 tsp. B. pdr.; ¼ tsp. soda; ¼ tsp. salt; 2/3 cup milk.

Cream butter, add sugar and cream some more — add well beaten egg, mix for a few seconds,

Add flour with baking powder and salt mixed in, alternately with the milk. Beat until smooth.

Grease heavy frying pan or griddle with a little butter.

Heat until medium heat.

Drop batter in teaspoons full (makes small 1½ to 2 inch fat pancake)

Cook until bubbles form, turn and cook until light brown. Butter and serve hot or cold or can be warmed up.

Betty' Filling for 1 doz - Frozen Tart Shell

1 cup - brown sugar

1 egg -

1 tablespoon vinegar - a little

½ teaspoon vanilla

raisins & nuts

¼ cup melted butter - added at last.

IX

Desserts, Puddings and Pastries

Making desserts for one can be a nuisance and you will probably settle for something out of a can, or preferably your own bottled fruit. Canned halves of peaches, apricots or pears are much more appetizing to finish your dinner with if you warm your portion for one in a little of the juice and an equal quantity of sherry; just let it come to simmer and not boil or you will evaporate that nice liquor. This can be done in one of the tiny white casseroles that you can use on top of your range.

The old fashioned way of making a rice pudding is a good thing when you have your oven on for one of those slow cooking, tough pot-roasty pieces of beef. See recipe —

GRANDMOTHER'S RICE PUDDING

1 tbsp. rice, wash it;
1 tbsp. br. sugar; 1 pint milk.

Stir into quart sized casserole and bake a long, long time in a very slow oven — 250 or so. When it comes up with a skin nicely yellowed stir it under. You will find you have to do this several times. The result is a most delicious creamy rice pudding. With cream and a very little sugar it is good either hot or cold.

ONE EGG CUSTARD

1 egg, beaten with a speck of salt;
1 tbsp. sugar, white or brown; add 1 c. milk.

Bake *slowly* in a small oven-heat bowl. Butter it. May be varied with a little nutmeg or powdered orange rind (Spice Island) sprinkled on top. It is done when a knife stuck into it comes out clean.

PASTRIES

Here are 2 easy ways of making small quantities of pastry which will keep for weeks if wrapped and kept in the refrigerator.

You can always bake a few tart shells, keep them in a tin and fill what you want to use at one time.

EASIEST PASTRY

½ c. pure lard; ½ tsp. salt;
¼ c. boiling water.

Stir together in medium sized bowl and let stand for one hour or less. Beat in

1½ c. flour and ½ tsp. B. Powder

Roll out and fold once or twice. Can be used for one pie or several tart shells, etc. May be rolled up in wax paper and kept in fridge for days.

NEVER FAIL PASTRY

Rub together:

1 c. lard; 2 heaping cups flour; ¼ tsp. baking powder; 1 level tbsp. yellow sugar; beat 1 egg lightly and add 1 tbsp. vinegar; ½ tsp. salt.

Do this in a measuring cup and then add cold water to make it about 3/8 full. May be a little mucky but roll in a ball and chill. May be kept for a couple of weeks, using as you require.

APPLES

If you are tired of the good old baked apple or little bread and apple pudding which your grandmother made, try one of these.

APPLES IN SYRUP

Make a thin syrup of (for one portion — but you will be wiser to make more as they are delicious cold):

½ c. sugar; 1 c. water;
3 thin slices of a lemon.

Add your quartered tart apples and let simmer until they are clear, don't cook until they break, please, and do *not* cover.

GERMAN APPLE CAKES

One or two of these with a cup of coffee or tea makes a nice dessert and you save a dish. The recipe makes six rather largish patty pans. The large size foil ones are good. The friend who gave it to me used scalloped aluminum jelly moulds.

Cream well: 1/3 c. butter and add gradually: ½ c. sugar and 1 egg; 1 c. flour sifted with 1 tsp. b. powder; ¼ tsp. salt and 3 tbsps. milk or "creamy".

Wedge in three or four wedges of peeled apple on top of each cake. Bake mod. oven 350 for 25 min. No spice and no sugar on top, please. Tart apples are delicious with crisp *butter* cake mix.

APPLE MERINGUE

1 large apple, peel and quarter;
1 wh. of a large egg; 1/3 c. of sugar.

Butter small casserole and arrange apples. Beat white of egg until very stiff, add the sugar and a pinch of salt.

Distribute this on top of apples and bake in a very slow oven until crisp all the way through.

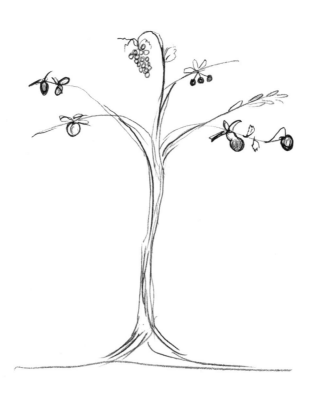

X

Cakes and Cookies

No one is going to be bothered baking cakes or cookies etc. for one and I know you all have dozens of pet recipes of your own, but I am giving you the cream of my crop of very best cakes, etc. over a long, long time.

All these are for cakes that keep well, maybe a little old fashioned, but made with as little trouble as possible.

DELICATE WHITE FRUIT CAKE

No spice, no raisins, no currants.
Cream well:

1 c. butter and add gradually 1 c. fruit sugar, cream again; 4 egg yolks, one at a time, cream again; 1 dessert spoon grated orange rind; 1 tsp. grated lemon rind; Juice ½ lemon; ½ orange; 2 c. sifted flour, (Velvet), reserve flour, (¼ cup) to sift on fruit. Fold in: 4 stiffly beaten whites of eggs; lastly: 1 pound, altogether, thinly sliced citron, orange, and lemon peel; 1 cup slivered, blanched almonds.

Should be baked 275 oven for three hours or more.

Nearly everyone who cooks and bakes her own cakes, etc. has a special pet and this is my very own. I bake it in largest size paper cups. They can be put in small "Baggies" and keep nicely for a week, or you may freeze them and they will keep for weeks.

SPICY RUM CAKES

1/3 c. butter, creamed with 1 c. yellow sugar; beat in: 1 egg; 1 tbsp. rum; ½ tsp. nutmeg; ½ tsp. ginger; 1 tsp. cinnamon; ¼ tsp. salt and cream together; Add: 1 large egg and cream together; 1½ c. all purpose flour, sifted well; 1½ tsp. B. Powder. Add flour alternately with ½ cup milk and 1 tsp. vanilla.

This makes about 20 paper cups. You may put a pecan on top of half of them before baking and on the other half when they come out of the oven put one of those thin chocolate-coated mints. It will melt and spread.

TAKE IT EASY CAKE

This recipe was given me by a friend and I have no other plain cake since, as it is so satisfactory and keeps well. Can be made in two small bread tins or in two layers.
In largest mixing bowl of set put:

2 c. presifted Velvet cake flour; 2½ tsp. B. Powder; 1 tsp. salt; 1¼ c. wh. sugar, all sifted together; add: ½ c. very soft butter (no skimping); 2/3 c. milk and 1 tsp. vanilla. Beat this two minutes by the clock and add, one at a time — 2 large unbeaten eggs.

Beat for one minute after each egg has been added. Bake in 350 oven for about 40 min. Sometimes I bake this in a ring mold and six paper cups. The cups you will probably gobble, they are so good, fresh out of the oven. You may wrap and freeze one loaf and it will keep fresh for a couple of weeks.

CHILDREN COMING COOKIES

Cream ½ c. butter; add ½ c. white sugar; ½ cup brown sugar; 1 egg; ¼ tsp. salt; 1 tsp. vanilla; 2/3 c. flour; ½ tsp. soda; 2 c. Special "K" breakfast food; 1 c. rice crispies; ½ c. chopped pecans.

Put walnut sized balls on greased bake sheet, flatten with a fork (should be about two inches apart).

Oven 325 until light brown. Watch.

PARTY MACAROONS

1 large egg white, beaten very stiffly; 1 c. brown and white sugar mixed; 1 c. ground almonds, skins on; ¼ tsp. almond flavouring; pinch of salt.

Bake in slow oven about 15 minutes.

Drop by dessert spoon on a cookie sheet, covered with wax paper. Remove as soon as baked as they stick.

SHORT BREAD COOKIES

Cream: 1 c. butter (½ lb.); add: ½ c. fruit sugar; pinch of soda; 1/8 tsp. salt; 2 c. all purpose flour.

Cream all well together and put in refrig. for an hour or so to firm.

Roll out — ½ inch thick, cut in rounds. Bake in a slow oven until a delicate tan.

SCOTCH SHORT BREAD

May be made the same as above, but substitute brown sugar for white sugar.

THIN OATMEAL COOKIES

These are very nice to eat with any kind of cheese and may be cut in triangles or squares and larger than ordinary cookies.

2 c. fine oatmeal; 2 tbsp. butter;
½ tsp. soda; ½ tsp. salt.

Just enough cold water to roll out into a very, very thin sheet. Bake in 350 oven about 10 minutes, or until they are a light tan.

HERMITS

Cream: 1 c. butter and add gradually; 1 c. wh. sugar; ½ c. br. sugar, beat in two eggs: 1½ tsp. freshly grated nutmeg; 1 tsp. cinnamon; ½ tsp. salt; 3 c. all purpose flour. When all mixed add: 1 c. chopped nice fresh dates; 1 c. raisins; 1 c. pecans or filberts.

So many packaged nuts, walnuts particularly, are stale and one bad one will spoil the flavour of your cookies.

Drop on cookie tins, two inches apart, and bake in 350 oven about 15 minutes.

These cookies are specially nice flavour and keep well.

Sadie's Cookies

Put 1 tablespoon butter in saucepan. Melt and add butterscotch pieces & then noodles (China L. Noodles). Drop teaspoonfuls on waxed paper.

XI

Breads and Buns

History tells us that bread was made thousands of years before the Christian Era.

It is one of our most important articles of food. Making one's own bread is by no means the task that so many women think it is.

There is nothing as appetizing as fresh home made bread or rolls and it is very much cheaper than the blown-up bakery or packaged products.

Methods of making are so much easier now than the old fashioned way of making the sponge over night and swathing it with a blanket to be kept warm — that anyone can have home baked bread with little effort.

The methods of making are very much the same and the most important rule to follow is to let the dough rise until double in bulk before putting in pans and again double in bulk before baking at 350 oven for 50 minutes. Turn out on rack. *Do not* rub crust with butter or cover with tea towel if you like a crisp crust.

BASIC BEST WHITE BREAD

This quantity of ingredients makes three loaves baked in regular 9½ x 5½ inch bread pans or four loaves in smaller 8½ by 4½ tins.

I find that 2½ cups of liquid will take 6 to eight cups of flour.

1 package dry yeast; 1 tsp. sugar, ½ cup lukewarm water; 1/3 cup sugar; 1 tbsp. salt; 2 tbsp. butter and 2 tbsp. pure lard; 1 cup boiling water; 1 cup cold water; 6 to 8 cups all purpose flour.

Dissolve yeast, 1 tsp. sugar and ½ c. lukewarm water in a mug or small bowl — it takes about ten minutes to rise.

Scald the butter, lard, sugar and salt with the cup of boiling water and stir to melt adding the other cup of water to cool to lukewarm. Place this in largest mixing bowl. *Add* the yeast mixture, stir well and beat in about five cups of the flour adding more to make a soft dough. Turn out on well floured board or cloth (I do mine on arborite sink top) and knead until smooth and elastic (too much flour will make the bread dry). Wash and grease bowl and replace bread, grease top, cover with a cloth. Let rise until it has doubled in bulk, it may take an hour.

Punch it down and let it rise once more to double in bulk when it may be kneaded down and divided into 3 large or 4 smaller loaves. Cover and let rise in pans until double in bulk and nicely rounded on top.

Bake in 375 oven until it is crisply light brown, from 45 to 60 minutes according to size of bread pan.

When I bake I give one loaf away, freeze 2 and work hard on the fourth.

Freeze in baggies and when you require a loaf take it out of freezing compartment and let it stand for an hour or so to thaw or place loaf in *paper bag* and put in 375 oven for ten minutes to warm. It will be just like freshly baked bread which ever way you do it.

This may be varied by using two cups of scalded milk and poured over shortening, salt and sugar, cooled to lukewarm before proceeding as above. Makes delicious *home-made* bread.

OVER NIGHT BREAD

This is a simple recipe and requires no kneading.

Soak 1 package fast rising yeast in
¾ cup warm water for 15 minutes.

Place seven cups of flour in a large mixing bowl and mix the following in as you would for pie crust.

2 tsps. salt; ½ c. W. sugar;
½ cup butter or margarine. Beat two eggs well, add 1½ cups cold milk.
Stir this into yeast mixture and add all flour and shortening mixture.

Mix this together until all is moistened, cover lightly and let rise over night in kitchen. No need to throw anything over it.

In the morning shape into buns or two loaves of bread, let rise and bake at 375 to 400. (twenty minutes for buns) 40 minutes for loaves. (Perhaps a little longer). Turn out of pans at once and cool on a rack.

One loaf may be frozen.

BROWN BREAD

In large bowl soak:

1 envelope yeast; 1 cup warm water.

When it has risen, stir and add:

2 tbsps. molasses; 1 tsp. salt; 2 tbsps. brown sugar;
1 c. warm water; 2 tbsps. melted butter.
Mix in:

3 cups whole wheat flour; 2 cups white flour — all purpose.

Beat and knead into a soft dough. Let rise until double in bulk. Knead down and form into two loaves. Let rise again until double in size. Bake at 375 to 400 for about an hour.
NOTE:
The recipe for *White bread* can be made with substitution of ½ cup Whole Wheat flour for White and gives a little more vitamin content.

MOLASSES BREAD

This recipe was given me just lately and is unusual and very nice.

1 package dry yeast dissolved in ¼ cup warm water in small container.

Place in large bowl

1¼ cups quick cooking oatmeal; ½ cup cornmeal, stir together; add 2 cups boiling water, beat well; add ½ cup of molasses; 2 tsps. salt; ¼ cup melted butter.

Cool to lukewarm, add the dissolved yeast and beat this all well, adding 4 to 5 cups flour. Knead until smooth. (It will be sticky). Let stand until it has doubled in bulk. Punch it down and let rise again. When light (it does not take long), make into three loaves (middle size), let rise until doubled in bulk and bake for one hour in a moderate oven 350. Turn out immediately on rack. Freezes well.

The following recipe makes a dozen fat buns. Start them early and you can have them for lunch.

FUNNY BUNS

In large mixing bowl:

2½ c. all purpose flour;

1 tbsp. sugar; 1 tsp. salt.

Soak one envelope dry yeast in ¼ cup water until light (about ten minutes) add yeast mixture to:

1 egg, beaten; 1 c. warm water;
2 level tbsps. melted butter.

If you have an electric mixer this can be made in largest bowl of set. (Hand electric mixer can be used in any large bowl).

Add liquid ingredients to bowl of flour etc. and beat until well mixed.

Let stand, uncovered, (it will be sticky), until it rises double in bulk.

Beat well and spoon out into a dozen large greased patty pans.

Let rise again until doubled in bulk and bake twenty minutes in 400 oven.

Turn out at once and they will be crisp. Do not cover while rising either time.

These are the lightest of all the refrigerator style rolls and easy to make as they require no kneading.

SALLY LUN

1 c. flour; ½ tsp. salt; 2 tsp. B. P.; ¼ c. butter; ¼ c. sugar. Rub together finely and add: 1 beaten egg with ½ c. milk.

Mix well and flatten out in a greased pie tin. Score in sixths and bake in hot oven 20 minutes.

CLOUD 9 ROLLS

Dissolve 1 pkg. dry yeast in

1 tsp. sugar; ¼ c. warm water.

In large bowl or cooking pot without handle place:

¼ c. butter; 1½ tsps. salt; 2 tbsp. sugar; 1 c. boiling water, stir until butter melts and mixture is lukewarm, add the dissolved yeast and 1 beaten egg, stir well and add 2¾ cups bread flour.

Beat until smooth and well mixed. Cover with a dinner plate and put in ice-box for a few hours or overnight. It should treble in bulk. About 3 hours before you require rolls break off small pieces and put two together in largest patty pans. Let rise in warm place for two hrs., or until well risen, (doubled, or more in size). Bake in 400 oven for about 20 minutes. May be frozen and heated in paper bag, 5 minutes in 400 oven.

Part of any bread dough can be cut off and made into a few buns or rolls, baked on a cookie sheet two inches apart so that you will have a crust all around or in large patty pans. The following recipes are explicitly for rolls and are the best of dozens of tried recipes.

REFRIGERATOR ROLLS

½ c. lard or butter and lard; 1 c. boiling water; ½ c. sugar. Cream shortening and sugar a little and add boiling water. Let cool to lukewarm. 2 envelopes dry yeast dissolved in 1 c. cold water; 1 tsp. sugar. Add to cooled first mixture with 2 eggs, beaten; 1 tsp. salt; 6 c. all purpose flour.

Beat in flour and mix well, cover bowl and put in refrigerator over night. Knead down and take out what you require for rolls. The remainder can be left in refrig for two or three days. Can be baked in muffin tins or shaped into oblong rolls, let rise two hrs. or more. Bake in 375 oven for twenty minutes.

The following recipes for Tea biscuits, Scones, Pancakes and Muffins are in small quantities and can be kept two or three days without freezing. They are all much preferable to packaged mixes and a great deal cheaper. All measurements are level.

TEA BISCUITS

Sift together 2 c. flour; 4 tsp. B. Powder; 1 tbsp. sugar; 1 tsp. salt. Cut in finely 1/3 c. butter or crisco. Add: 1 beaten egg with ¾ c. milk.

Mix lightly and turn out on floured surface. Pat into about an inch thickness and cut with largest cookie cutter. Place on cookie sheet an inch apart and bake in hot oven, about 400 for 12 min.

XII

Doctor's Orders

What could be better for the ending of this little book than the following recipe, taken from a hundred year old cook book and tried several times with extremely beneficial results;

DR. BECKERSTITHS RESTORATIVE

12 newly laid eggs; Juice of 12 lemons;
½ pound of Rock candy; 1 pint of first class rum

Place eggs in large rather shallow bowl, being *very* careful not to crack them. Let *lemons* stand in hot water for a few minutes and roll them well (you will get twice as much juice from them). Pour the lemon juice over the dry eggs and candy and let stand for nine days in ice box. Keep the bowl covered and turn eggs carefully each day being careful *not* to crack or crush them.

At the end of nine days whisk well (the shells will be practically dissolved). Strain, add the rum and bottle. Dose — take a small wine glass full once a day. This is truly a wonderful *tonic* — try to say "DR. Beckerstiths Restorative" rapidly three times — after you have had a wee glass (or two).

Freda's. Strawberry Jam
1 quart strawberries, wash and drain
Place 1 quart sugar. (same amt. sugar)
1 tablespoon cold water
Boil well 10 minutes

Index

Almost Instant Cheese Sauce 19

Apple(s) 22, 50, 52-53
  Cakes, German 53
  and celery salad 22
  meringue 53
  pancakes 50
  in syrup 52

Asparagus 45

Aunt Lizzie's Chicken Salad 23

Beans, baked 45

Beef 37-43
  Carbonnade de 40
  hamburger 37
    curried 40
  Shepherd's Pie 38
  steak 42
    broiled............................ 42
      new method 42
    Creole Round 42
    lazy 37
  stew 41
    quickie 41

Beet(s) 22, 46
  baked.................................. 46
  and celery salad 22

Biscuits, tea 60

Bread(s)......................... 48, 57-59
  brown 58
  baked bread and cheese
    custard 48
  molasses 59
  Over Night 58
  white, best basic 57

Breading 12

Broccoli 46

Buns (see rolls) 59

Butter, seasoned 25

Cabbage, digestible 46

Caper and sour cream sauce 18

Cake(s) 53-55
  fruit cake, delicate white 54
  German Apple 53
  Rum, Spicy........................... 54
  Take It Easy 55

Carbonnade de Boeuf 40

Carrots, baked 46

Cheese 19, 33, 35, 48-49
  custard 48
  Old Fashioned Welsh Rarebit 49
  omelette 33
  with poached eggs 35
  sauce 19
    Almost Instant 19
    instant 19
  soufflé 35

Chicken................................. 26-30
  about 26
  à la king 29
    sauce for 30
  breast, with lemon juice 28
  Chinese 28
  fricasee 27
  fried 27
    modern 27
    old fashioned 27
  Gingery Legs and Thighs 27
  Makeshift Lazy 28
  marinated 29
  Salad, Aunt Lizzie's 23

Children Coming Cookies 55

Chinese Chicken 28

Clam chowder 14

Cloud 9 Rolls 60

Cookies 55-56
  Children Coming 55
  Hermits 56
  macaroons, party 55
  oatmeal, thin 56
  short bread 55
    Scotch 56

Corn 47

Corned Beef 24, 43
    hash 43
    salad supper 24

Cottage cheese and fruit salad ... 23

Crab 15, 16
    hot weather supper 15
    Norahburg 16

Creole Round Steak 42

Croutons, home made 25

Cucumber sauce 19

Curry 13, 15, 35, 39-40
    curried eggs 35
    curried scallops 13
    Indian 39
    quick 40
    sauce 15

Custard(s) 48, 51
    baked bread and cheese 48
    delicate cheese 48
    one egg 51
    steamed cheese 48

Desserts 49-56
    about 51
    cakes 53-55
    custards 51
    meringues 53
    pancakes 49-50
    pastries 52
    puddings 51

Dr. Beckerstith's Restorative 61

Dressings 15, 21-22
    (see also vinegars)
    French, basic 22
    Italian, basic 22
    mayonnaise.......................... 21
    salad 21-22
    sea food with avocado 15
    sour cream 21

Dumplings 41

Egg(s) 31-36
    baked 34
       with mustard 34
    boiled 31
       hard 31
    curried 35
    custard............................... 51
    omelettes 32-34
    pickled 36
    poached 35
    scrambled 34
    soufflés 35
    stuffed 36

Entrées 48-49

Fish............................... 11-15
    (see specific fish)
    about 11

    breaded 12
    broiled 11
    cakes 12
    creamed 15
    fillet or slice of 12

French dressing, basic 22

Fruit 23, 54
    cake, delicate white 54
    salad, with cottage cheese 23

Funny Buns 59

Garlic vinegar 20

German Apple Cakes 53

Gingery Legs and Thighs 27

Grandmother's Rice Pudding 51

Ham and egg salad 24

Hermits 56

Hungarian veal cutlet 39

Indian curry 39

Italian dressing, basic 22

Jane's Scotch Tea Pancakes 50

Liver, delicious 40

Lobster Norahburg 16

Makeshift Lazy Chicken 28

Mayonnaise 18, 21
    sour cream 18
    real commercial 21

Meat 37-38
    (see also specific meats)
    patties, gourmet 38

Molasses bread 59

Mushroom(s) 18, 33
    omelette 33
    soup, cream of 18

Nasturtium vinegar 20

Never Fail Pastry 52

Omelettes 31-34
    cheese 33
    filled 32
    fresh mushroom 33
    left over anything 34
    plain 32
    tomato 33
    tomato and cheese 33
    use of water in 32

Onion poach 35

Orange sour cream sauce 18

Over Night Bread 58

Oysters 13-14
    fried 13
       with bacon 13
       gourmet 13
    quick gourmet 14
    scalloped 14

Pancakes 49-50
    apple 50
    bread crumb 49
    Jane's Scotch Tea 50
    potato 49
    Very Daring 50
    yeast 49

Papaya seed vinegar 21

Parsley 19

Pastry(ies) 52
    about 52
    easiest 52
    Never Fail 52

Pork 38-39
    parcel dinner 38
    spareribs 39
    tenderloin 39

Potato(es) 23, 44-45, 49
    baked 44
    creamed, quick 45
    french fried, pretend 45
    pan broiled, quick 45
    pancakes 49
    salad 23
    scalloped, pretend 44

Pudding(s) 51
    rice, grandmother's 51

Rolls 59-60
    Cloud 9 60
    Funny Buns 59
    refrigerator 60
    Sally Lun 59

Rum Cakes, Spicy 54

Salad(s) 22-24
    apple and celery 22
    Aunt Lizzie's Chicken 23
    beet and celery 22
    corned beef salad supper 24
    cottage cheese and fruit 23
    dressings 21, 22
    easy salad supper 24
    ham and egg 24
    potato 23

Sally Lun 59

Salmon, broiled fresh slice 12

Sauce(s) 15, 18-19, 24, 30
    Almost Instant Cheese 19
    for chicken à la king 30
    cucumber 19
    curry 15
    horse radish 24
    instant cheese 19
    orange sour cream 18
    seafood with sour cream 18
    sour cream and caper 18

Scallops 13
    breaded 13
    curried 13

Shellfish (see specific shellfish)

Scotch Short Bread 56

Sheperd's Pie 38

Short bread 55-56
    cookies 55
    Scotch 56

Shrimp 15-16
    hot weather supper 15
    Norahburg 16

Soufflé, cheese 35

Soup(s) 14, 17-18
    about 17
    clam chowder 14
    cream, basic 17
    cream of mushroom 18

Sour Cream 18,21
    and caper sauce 18
    dressing 21
    mayonnaise 18
    and orange sauce 18

Spareribs 39

Spicy Rum Cakes 54

Stews 41
    beef 41
      quickie 41

Syrup, apples in 52

Take It Easy Cake 50

Tarragon vinegar 20

Tea biscuits 60

Tomato(es) 25, 33-34, 47
    and cheese omelette 34
    dressed up 25
    fried 47
      cornmeal 47
    omelette 33
    slices 47

Tonic 61

Veal 39
    bird 39
    cutlet, Hungarian 39

Vegetables 44-47
    (see also specific vegetables)
    about 44

Very Daring Pancakes 50

Vinegar(s)......................... 20-21
    garlic 20
    nasturtium 20
    papaya seed 21
    seasoned 20
    tarragon 20

Welsh Rarebit, Old Fashioned 49